FINTECH AND THE FUTURE OF FINANCE

FINTECH AND THE FUTURE OF FINANCE

MARKET AND POLICY IMPLICATIONS

Erik Feyen, Harish Natarajan, Matthew Saal

CONTENTS

FIGURES

MAPS

TABLE

FOREWORD

The monumental challenges we face today, from COVID-19 (coronavirus) to the war in Ukraine, have reminded us that throughout history, turbulent times are often accompanied by innovation.

The technology-enabled innovation in financial services—known as *fintech*—is one such example, accelerating rapidly as pandemic shutdowns amplified its importance for maintaining business activity and financial services during a time of social distancing.

Every day, headlines attest to the seismic shifts that fintech is bringing to the financial services industry, driven by a dramatic expansion of internet access and smartphone use, combined with lower-cost computing and data storage. As financial products, payments, and business models evolve—even the concept of money itself—so too are market players and the structure of the markets in which they compete. Large telecommunications and information technology companies, retail chains, and small start-up companies are joining traditional banks and nonfinancial institutions in providing services.

Digital financial services can play a significant role in maintaining active credit markets to support a resilient and inclusive recovery, leveraging data, analytics, and new business models such as embedded finance. They can also create new opportunities to make the global financial system more efficient and inclusive by overcoming geographic and physical obstacles to services and by making information more widely available to consumers and providers.

Policy makers globally have embraced fintech development to promote innovation and growth of the digital economy. For regulators and supervisors, however, digital transformation has also created challenges in balancing innovations with the safeguarding of competition, financial stability and integrity, consumer protection, and data privacy.

To help inform policy makers in navigating a complex financial system, this publication explores the digital transformation under way in financial services and the implications of fintech for market outcomes as well as regulation and supervision. It looks at the range of new market providers, business models, and products that have amplified the need for updated legal, regulatory, and supervisory frameworks.

This work builds on the World Bank Group's efforts to support financial innovation at all levels. The World Bank has been supporting governments in adapting regulatory frameworks, modernizing systems and other financial infrastructure, and ensuring high standards of consumer protection. The International Finance Corporation has been investing in a diverse group of private sector fintech providers for over a decade, promoting the growth of responsible, inclusive finance providers that serve tens of millions of customers across global emerging markets.

The World Bank Group and the International Monetary Fund launched the Bali Fintech Agenda in 2018, recognizing the need for regulators and policy makers to actively engage as technology transforms finance, to take advantage of new efficiencies and opportunities to broaden financial access and achieve financial inclusion while safeguarding financial stability and consumer protection.

Amid the continuing efforts to recover losses from ongoing crises, expanding access to financial services is one way to support businesses and get communities back on track. For poor people and microenterprises, the use of basic services such as transaction accounts enables them to send and receive payments securely and gain access to savings, credit, and insurance products that can help them plan for hard times, invest in their futures, and grow their businesses.

We hope that this publication will be a useful guide for policy makers around the world as they seek to manage the long-standing risks and maximize the economic and social benefits of financial innovation.

Mari E. Pangestu
Managing Director of Development Policy and Partnerships
The World Bank

ACKNOWLEDGMENTS

Fintech and the Future of Finance distills the key findings and messages of a series of technical notes jointly developed by the World Bank and the International Financial Corporation (IFC).

This project was led by Erik Feyen and Harish Natarajan (both World Bank) and Matthew Saal (IFC), under the overall guidance of Jean Pesme, Anderson Caputo Silva, and Mahesh Uttamchandani (all World Bank) and Paulo de Bolle and Martin Holtmann (both IFC). Alfonso García Mora (IFC, formerly World Bank) provided guidance at the inception and earlier stages of the report.

The team of authors of the technical notes comprised Tatiana Alonso Gispert, Oya Ardic, Gian Boeddu, Ana M. Carvajal, Pierre-Laurent Chatain, Jennifer Chien, Dorothee Delort, Tatiana Didier, Matei Dohotaru, Karl Driessen, Erik Feyen, Jose Antonio Garcia Garcia Luna, Ivor Istuk, Ruth Llovet Montañés, Harish Natarajan, Danilo Palermo, Ariadne Plaitakis, Guillermo Galicia Rabadan, and Arpita Sarkar (all World Bank); Robert Paul Heffernan, Luis Maldonado, Matthew Saal, Miguel Soriano, Ghada Teima, and John Wilson (all IFC); and Giulio Cornelli, Jon Frost, Leonardo Gambacorta, and Tara Rice (all Bank for International Settlements).

The team appreciates comments provided on this report by Bob Cull and Martin Raiser (World Bank); Andi Dervishi, Neil Gregory, Hans Koning, and Nathalie Louat (IFC); and Aditya Narain (International Monetary Fund).

The team thanks Machimanda A. Deviah (World Bank) for editorial assistance; Maria Lopez (World Bank) and Sensical Design for design; Elizabeth Price, Melissa Knutson, and Nandita Roy (all World Bank) and Henry Pulizzi and Elena Gex (both IFC) for communications support; and Michael Geller and Arpita Sarkar (both World Bank) for overall coordination.

MAIN MESSAGES

Fintech, the application of digital technology to financial services, is reshaping the future of finance. Digital technologies are revolutionizing payments, lending, investment, insurance, and other financial products and services—a process that the COVID-19 pandemic has accelerated. In 2018 the World Bank Group and the International Monetary Fund launched the Bali Fintech Agenda, a set of 12 policy elements aimed at helping member countries to harness the benefits and opportunities of rapid advances in financial technology that are transforming the provision of banking services while at the same time managing the inherent risks.

Digitalization of financial services and money is helping to bridge gaps in access to financial services for households and firms and is promoting economic development

The latest World Bank Global Findex data show that global financial account ownership grew from 51 percent of the adult population in 2011 to 76 percent in 2021. Access to basic financial services such as savings, insurance, and credit translates into better firm productivity and growth for micro and small businesses, as well as higher incomes and resilience, to improve the lives of the poor. Yet too many people and firms still lack access to essential financial services that could help them thrive.

Technology can lower transaction costs by overcoming geographical access barriers; increasing the speed, security, and transparency of transactions; and allowing for more tailored financial services that better serve consumers, including the poor. Women can especially benefit. Therefore, countries should embrace fintech opportunities and implement policies that enable and encourage safe financial innovation and adoption.

Fintech is transforming the financial sector landscape rapidly and profoundly, calling for the active engagement of policy makers

Fintech is making an impact in many countries. Examples include the rapid ascent of mobile money, bank apps, financial services provided by Big Tech firms and neobanks, and crypto-assets and central bank digital currencies. New infrastructures, providers, products, and business models are reshaping market structures in profound ways (market developments, as discussed further in appendix A). These technological advances are blurring the boundaries of both financial firms and the financial sector. For example, financial firms more often rely on third parties to offer their products and services, and nonfinancial firms are increasingly embedding financial services into their products.

In addition to inclusion, core policy objectives for a well-functioning financial system include financial stability and integrity; efficiency, which is linked to fair competition; cyber and operational soundness and security; data privacy; and consumer and investor protection. Allowing fintech developments to be driven solely by market forces would compromise these objectives. For example, economies of scale and scope could lead to market concentration, with adverse consequences for competition, innovation, and financial stability.

Policy makers must adapt

As the financial sector continues to transform, policy trade-offs will evolve. It is important to ensure that market outcomes remain aligned with core policy objectives. Several policy recommendations emerge:

- *Manage risks while fostering beneficial innovation and competition.* Given the fast-evolving landscape and rapid spread of innovation, a regulatory approach that supports responsible fintech innovation and adoption is critical. Prudential supervision, market conduct, and consumer protection agencies should coordinate extensively as fintech issues cut across their mandates. Regulators should strive to promote trust and investment and minimize exposing consumers, particularly the poor, to undue risks. This will require regulators to be proactive, pragmatic, and clear in their decisions.

- *Broaden monitoring horizons and reassess regulatory perimeters.* Financial services are increasingly provided by a wide variety of entities and are even embedded into commercial transactions and social interactions. These developments blur the boundaries of the financial sector. It is essential to proactively monitor the comprehensive financial sector value chain and reshape the regulatory perimeter accordingly.

- *Review regulatory, supervisory, and oversight frameworks.* The range of new products and providers, the use of new technologies and a wider range of data, and the inclusion of new customer segments in increasingly complex markets has made existing regulatory and supervisory mandates and approaches insufficient. Principles that help underpin policies include pursuing an approach that is proportional to risks; maintaining a level playing field by treating the same activities and risks similarly, looking through technology and focusing on underlying economic functions; and ensuring the primacy of core policy objectives. This may call for tailored approaches that are entity based.

- *Be mindful of evolving policy trade-offs as fintech adoption deepens.* As fintech continues to permeate the financial sector, policy decisions will entail trade-offs that call for attention to proper safeguards to maintain financial stability and fair competition, ensure data and consumer protection, and prevent the abuse of market power. Regulators can better balance the trade-offs between stability, competition, concentration, efficiency, and inclusion through various actions, including:

- Formulating data collection principles and proactively monitoring market conduct

- Establishing frameworks for open banking and data ownership

- Revisiting restrictions on product tying and linkages between banking and commerce.

- *Monitor market structure and conduct to maintain competition.* The initial focus of many regulators has been on facilitating market entry since small start-ups and new entrants have been driving the momentum of innovation. However, the industry is rapidly boomeranging toward concentration of players and platforms because of the economies of scale and the massive amounts of data held by Big Tech companies. These developments may deliver inclusion and efficiency, particularly in low- and middle-income economies that may lack a robust, competitive, and inclusive banking sector. However, regulators will need to proactively monitor markets and dynamically balance trade-offs between competition, concentration, efficiency, data protection, and inclusion.

- *Modernize and open financial infrastructure.* Financial infrastructure may need upgrading to enable digital products and services. Infrastructure should be interoperable and open to both new and traditional players. The increasing role of fintech companies, embedded finance by Big Tech companies, digital money, and cross-border financial flows will pressure regulators to ensure that the access policies of financial infrastructures are fair and transparent. Moreover, with the entry of new market-level services that take on characteristics of financial infrastructures, regulators will need to assess whether and how to bring them within the regulatory perimeter.

- *Ensure that public money remains fit for the digital world.* Reduced reliance on public money could impede authorities from shaping and safeguarding financial sector and economic development. The ongoing digitization of the economy and payments, the world of crypto-assets, and the influence of Big Tech firms in payments and user data, over time, could challenge the role of public money, competition, and privacy. Public authorities might consider distinct, public alternatives to crypto-assets, such as central bank digital currencies (CBDCs), in addition to strengthening policy frameworks regarding crypto-assets and Big Tech firms. Countries that consider creating a CBDC should carefully evaluate the wide-ranging implications and design options in consultation with public and private stakeholders.

- *Pursue strong cross-border coordination and sharing of information and best practices.* Fintech developments enable providers to reach a wide set of customers across borders and provide services without necessarily being subject to regulation in the customer's jurisdiction. Regulators and public authorities need to collaborate and coordinate with their peers to safeguard their respective financial systems and customers.

ABBREVIATIONS

AI	artificial intelligence
AML/CFT	anti-money laundering and combating the financing of terrorism
API	application programming interface
ATM	automated teller machine
BaaS	banking as a service
B2B	business-to-business
CBDC	central bank digital currency
COVID-19	coronavirus disease
DeFi	decentralized finance
DFS	digital financial services
DLT	distributed ledger technology
eKYC	electronic Know Your Customer
EMDEs	emerging markets and developing economies
FCP	financial consumer protection
fintech	financial technology
FSB	Financial Stability Board
FSP	financial service provider
GDP	gross domestic product
ICT	information and communication technology
ID	identification
IMF	International Monetary Fund
IT	information technology

KYC	Know Your Customer
NBFI	nonbank financial institution
PSP	payment service provider
P2P	peer-to-peer
P2PL	peer-to-peer lending
QR	quick response
SaaS	software as a service
SIM	subscriber identity module
SMEs	small and medium enterprises
USSD	Unstructured Supplementary Service Data

Overview

Introduction

The ongoing digitization of financial services and money creates opportunities to build more inclusive and efficient financial services and promote economic development. Countries should embrace these opportunities and implement policies that enable and encourage safe financial innovation and adoption. Technological advances are blurring the boundaries of both financial firms and the financial sector. New infrastructures, providers, products, business models, and market structures are shaping market outcomes in profound ways. As such, it is necessary to ensure that market outcomes remain aligned with core policy objectives as the financial sector continues to transform and policy trade-offs evolve.

This flagship publication explores the implications of financial technology (fintech) and the digital transformation of financial services for market outcomes, on the one hand, and the regulation and supervision of financial services, on the other hand, and explores how these interact. It provides a high-level perspective for senior policy makers and is accompanied by a set of technical notes that focus in detail on selected salient issues for a more technical audience (as listed and summarized in appendix B of this publication). Figure O.1 lays down a conceptual framework for fintech and the interactions between markets, policy, and development.

FIGURE O.1 **Conceptual Framework for Fintech: Interactions between Markets, Policy, and Development**

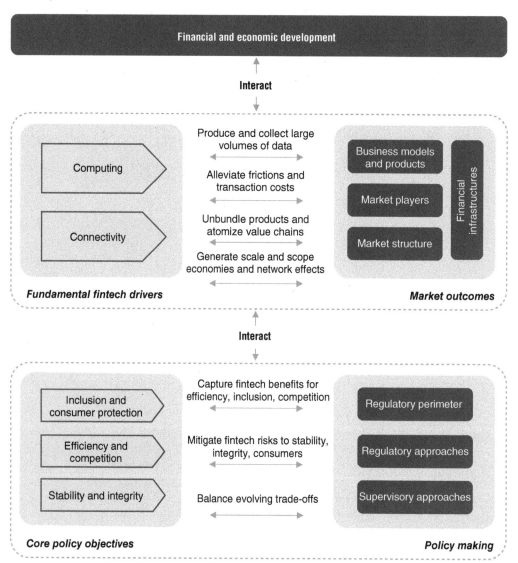

Source: Original elaboration for this publication.

The Fundamental Drivers of Fintech

Technology-enabled innovation in financial services—fintech—is reshaping financial products, payments, business models, market players, market structure, and even money itself. This is a global phenomenon, especially in the realm of payments, according to the global patterns examined in the Fintech Activity Note developed for this publication (Didier et al. 2022). The adoption of fintech was accelerated by the COVID-19 pandemic (further discussed in appendix C).

Fintech adoption can further financial development by promoting core policy objectives such as financial stability, integrity, inclusion, efficiency, innovation, and competition, and it can provide the firm foundations needed for the digital economy to flourish. Fintech-enabled business models and products can support economies to become more resilient and promote an equitable recovery from the pandemic (World Bank 2022). At the same time, a balanced policy approach is required to mitigate various risks related to, among others, financial stability and integrity, consumer and investor protection, fair competition, and data privacy—further addressed in the Consumer Protection Note prepared for this publication (Boeddu and Chien 2022).

The two fundamental drivers of this wave of fintech are (a) ubiquitous connectivity through mobile, internet-connected devices and communication networks; and (b) low-cost computing and data storage. Together, these enable new business models for the delivery of technology such as cloud computing. Applications leveraging these advances, such as e-commerce and mobile apps, create reams of Big Data about users and transactions. Low-cost computing and storage allow that data to be mined for insights.

Reducing frictions in financial services. These drivers—data and connectivity—can alleviate key frictions in the provision of financial services, such as information asymmetries and transactions costs. They have therefore enabled a wide range of data-driven process automation and product applications, from credit and insurance underwriting to investment robo-advisors.

Data-driven business models are able to scale rapidly, leveraging positive feedback loops from customer activity that generates data that are used to provide additional services, which, in turn, generate more user engagement and data. Lenders that previously relied on a borrower's credit history or collateral to fill information gaps about cash flows and ability to repay can now use data-driven credit scores and real-time payments data on cash flows to extend credit to previously underserved individuals and small and medium enterprises (SMEs), reaching them at a lower cost through mobile channels.

Atomizing the value chain. These drivers also enable the reconfiguration of the value chains that produce financial services. Transaction costs and barriers to information flows have long defined the scope of what was produced within a single firm; reduced transaction costs and friction-free information flows allow a reconfiguration of financial services value chains and product bundles. Connectivity and data exchange allow a product or service to be broken up into distinct components (atomization) that can be offered by different providers and recombined in new ways.

Account opening, for example, has moved from being a single-provider service delivered at the bank branch, using its own front and back offices, to a range of potential configurations. Now, a bank account might be opened either through its physical locations or through the mobile app of a partner such as a retailer or an e-commerce platform, with identification (ID) verification provided by a specialized fintech, the ledger sitting on an outsourced cloud-based information technology (IT) infrastructure, and customer service provided by an offshore call center. That account might be branded as a bank product, or it might be delivered by the partner as a service "powered by" the partner with the consumer barely aware of the underlying financial institution.

Unbundling and rebundling services. The ability of customers and providers to access information and move funds more easily has enabled the unbundling of financial services: specialized providers offer single products, and customers can choose a set of service providers that collectively meets their needs. Rather than using the deposit, payment, and loan products of a single institution, customers can choose to keep deposits in one place (or more), shop around for the best loan offer, and use different payments providers for different uses—paying bills, splitting a restaurant bill, or sending money overseas. Customers can now assemble their own sets of services and bundle them at the level of app icons on a smartphone screen.

Critically, the same advances in computing power, data, and connectivity allow service providers—which do not own the whole customer financial relationship (as banks once did)—to provide single solutions and new packages of financial services or to rebundle financial services with other business or commercial activities.

Reshaping business models. Atomization, unbundling, and rebundling are reshaping business models and product economics as well as the provider landscape. An account holder might choose a third-party application for remote access to an account, effectively separating the account-holding institution from the end product and user interface—and much of the consumer value creation.

Economywide trends—such as wider use of application programming interfaces (APIs) in technology architecture and the rise of multiparty platforms in e-commerce, logistics, and other sectors—further enable information exchanges and the rebundling of financial services, which are being embedded into non-financial products and workflows. The introduction of variable and on-demand (cloud-based) infrastructure, automation, remote channels, and capital-light and embedded business models is reducing costs to customers. The new array of customer-facing providers will, however, take some of the margin that was previously earned by banks, even where regulation may still require that a bank be behind the product.

Market Outcomes

Although the digital transformation of the financial sector remains a work in progress, it is already changing financial infrastructures, products, and business models, bringing new entrants and reshaping incumbents and market structure. Customer behavior is changing, and competition is increasing. There is the potential to vastly improve financial inclusion, particularly in emerging markets and developing economies (EMDEs), by overcoming physical and geographic barriers to access to, and closing the information gaps on, credit and other products. Incumbents and entrants alike assign strategic priority to digitizing customer channels, internal processes, and product adoption. Market outcomes will ultimately depend on a variety of factors, including the scale and scope of economies; the customer preferences for choice versus convenience; and the policy framework, including regulatory approaches to licensing, data, and competition.

New Financial Infrastructures

Digital transformation creates a need for new infrastructures—such as fast payment systems, digital ID, and data exchange platforms—to support the other market outcomes. It also provides new ways to meet that need. The impact of changing financial infrastructure may be largest in EMDEs, where prior infrastructures are most lacking. Financial infrastructures are no longer the sole purview of the central bank, incumbent payment system operators, and authorized credit bureaus or asset registries.

In more developed markets, advances in connectivity between bank systems have enabled faster payments, and these advances are now increasingly being adopted in EMDEs as well. Further, in EMDEs, mobile money systems are filling a gap in access to retail accounts and payments, enabling individuals to easily transact at a distance and SMEs to accept digital payments, as discussed in detail in the Payments Note developed for this publication (Delort and Garcia Luna 2022). Mobile money systems have become a significant component of the payments landscape and are taking on some of the functions usually associated with financial infrastructure.

In Estonia and India, government-provided digital IDs have become part of the foundational infrastructure for access to financial and other services. In most countries, digital ID-verification services are layered on top of existing nondigital government IDs by private sector innovators. Technology has expanded the potential coverage and impact of other existing infrastructures as well, such as credit information and collateral registries.

Further, technological developments have opened the door for new quasi-infrastructure solutions, including innovative providers of alternative data credit scoring and industry-led factoring and reverse factoring platforms. As technology enables a broader range of providers to offer financial services, both traditional financial infrastructures and quasi-financial infrastructures play essential roles for new entrants and incumbents seeking to participate in the market—giving rise, however, to potential challenges related to competition, pricing, and fair access.

Innovation in Both Broadened and Niche Markets

Technology enables providers to serve and profit from broader markets as well as defined market segments. Digital channels for financial services enable providers to reach a broader market without the need for a high-cost branch infrastructure. The low-cost reach of digital banks paired with customers' ability to search digitally for services enables focused providers to find and serve a dispersed niche customer segment. Automated data-driven processes can serve low-value, high-volume segments efficiently and profitably.

Products also can be configured and tailored to meet the specific needs of a particular consumer or business segment, enabling, for example, the provision to SMEs of products like trade finance, invoice discounting, and foreign exchange services that were once reserved for high-volume large corporates, as found in the SME Note prepared for this publication (Teima et al. 2022). Moreover, the growth of affinity digital banks serving the specific needs of segments—such as freelancers and gig workers; artists and musicians; or lesbian, gay, bisexual, transgender, and queer (LGBTQ) customers—demonstrates that product tailoring and eliminating geographic constraints can enable the assembly of a viable customer base within even a narrow market segment. These business model and product innovations are building on mobile access to drive meaningful financial inclusion, making available a wider range of products and services that are appropriate for previously excluded retail and SME market segments.

Technology has enabled niche providers to be economically viable; however, even in the digital age, classic economies of scale and scope remain strong forces, and convenience and trust still matter to consumers. Economies of scale and scope, as well as network effects in customer acquisition and servicing and data production and use, increasingly drive digital business models. These forces confer advantages on providers with larger customer bases, such as Big Tech platforms. Scale and scope economies encourage a rebundling of financial services; they allow diversified fintech and Big Tech companies and other new players to deepen their inroads in core financial products.

Furthermore, although unbundling gives users more choice, they must also weigh the time, effort, and monetary costs of searching for and assembling individual financial services from different providers. Consumers continue to prize simplicity, convenience, and trust—factors that favor brand names and large players offering a broad range of products. Providers will therefore optimize their comparative advantages in technology, skills, reputation, capital, customer base, and other assets to determine how to position themselves along the spectrum from single service within a product value chain, to single product provider, to broad multiproduct player.

This strategic positioning—as either a focused niche provider or as a large, multi product provider—could lead to a "barbell" market structure outcome, as noted in the Market Structure Note prepared for this publication (Feyen et al. 2022a). The resulting market configuration would be one of large banks and fintech and Big Tech firms coexisting with a competitive tail of targeted niche firms. Many firms are making strategic decisions consistent with this market path, as evidenced by the continued entry of new players alongside the trend toward rebundling, including fintech firms seeking banking licenses. Ecosystems in which small providers can thrive by connecting independently to customers, or through partnerships with platforms for which they fill product or service gaps, can enable persistence of this bimodal market.

The Decentralized Frontier: Crypto-Assets

Crypto-assets, including stablecoins and decentralized finance (DeFi), offer new opportunities, as well as significant challenges. Technology is blurring one of the last functional boundaries: the distinction between an individual and a financial intermediary, as discussed in the Digital Money Note prepared for this publication (Feyen et al. 2022b). Distributed ledger and similar technologies underpin new, decentralized financial infrastructures that reduce or remove the role of intermediaries, enabling users to interact directly on a peer-to-peer basis and providing open-source platforms that anybody can use and build on, spurring innovation and network effects and giving rise to new, interoperable financial services and vibrant ecosystems.

Crypto-assets, including stablecoins and DeFi, are distributed ledger technology (DLT)-based, decentralized forms of digital value and financial services that aim to serve a range of economic functions. They hold promise for financial innovation, inclusion, efficiency, capital formation, and transparency. For example, they could improve the speed and cost of cross-border payments and remittances, which are key for EMDEs. However, these new technologies carry significant risks related to, among others, financial integrity, consumer and investor protection, financial stability, fair competition, and monetary sovereignty.

Policy Objectives and Roles for Policy Makers

Allowing fintech developments to be driven solely by market forces may ultimately not serve core policy objectives. These objectives include promoting financial innovation, efficiency, and inclusion while mitigating risks associated with financial stability and integrity; cyber and operational risks; data, consumer, and investor protection; fair competition; and cross-border regulatory arbitrage.

The technology that enables niche providers to be economically viable by targeting a particular product or segment does not ensure open and competitive markets. The simultaneous tendency toward market concentration, particularly due to economies of scale and network effects in data, raises concerns about potential anticompetitive conduct, even as it may also deliver inclusion and efficiency, particularly in developing economies that lack competitive and inclusive financial sectors. A concentrated provider or a Big Tech crossing over into finance may provide financial services that are otherwise unavailable. Consumers can benefit from a wave of fintech-induced innovation and competition even as markets become more concentrated. In this environment, proper policy safeguards become increasingly important for maintaining fair competition and preventing abuse of market power. Similarly, crypto-assets and DeFi ecosystems could reduce costs and spur innovation, but they currently lack transparency and adequate investor, consumer, and financial integrity protections.

Balancing the Trade-Offs

Policy trade-offs may evolve as fintech adoption increases. This dynamic can make it more challenging to ensure that market outcomes remain aligned with core policy objectives. At lower levels of fintech development, providing basic policy support for innovation and mitigating immediate risks—such as illicit activity and protection of customer funds—may yield good short-term outcomes as policy makers aim to reap innovation, inclusion, and efficiency gains.

Consumers have benefited from a wave of fintech-induced innovation and competition even as markets have become more concentrated. Policy makers, however, must remain aware that adoption can increase rapidly; they will need to improve their monitoring tools and be ready to step in. Strengthening or clarifying policy frameworks and improving financial infrastructures become increasingly important to continuing to safely support fintech adoption as (a) fintech reaches more consumers, increasing its volume and dependence on user data, and (b) certain providers reach scale.

Some EMDEs have adapted regulatory and supervisory frameworks in response to fintech developments, although market participants indicate there is further scope for improvement, as further discussed in chapter 5 and the Regulation Note developed for this publication (Gispert et al. 2022). To bring fintech activities within the regulatory perimeter, various EMDEs have applied or adapted existing regulatory frameworks or developed bespoke regulations or "sandboxes" to promote safe innovation. Some countries have done so after a period of observing industry developments and letting some fintech activities go unregulated. This approach may entail risk.

Countries also feel the need to evaluate the appropriateness of their supervisory frameworks as the financial sector undergoes digital transformation. According to the Fintech Market Participants Survey conducted for this report, supervisors will need to catch up, particularly in EMDEs (Feyen et al. 2022c). Many EMDEs need to strengthen their approach to addressing the consequences of fintech failures, although special wind-down procedures are only indicated in cases where the provider has systemic relevance. Many high-income economies are adopting comprehensive data protection and privacy frameworks, while EMDEs typically lag.

Managing the Crypto-Asset Environment

Most policy makers have taken a cautious stance regarding crypto-assets and issued public warnings regarding the risks. Many jurisdictions aim to provide an environment for safe innovation and adoption; they are clarifying existing legal, regulatory, and supervisory approaches or creating new ones. At the same time, the Central African Republic and El Salvador have adopted bitcoin as legal tender, while other jurisdictions have limited or banned some or all crypto-assets activities.

In light of their supranational and decentralized nature, crypto-assets pose domestic and international regulatory arbitrage risks. Various standard-setting bodies are applying general and transparent principles to provide guidance, set minimum requirements, and promote cross-border collaboration. In doing so, they need to focus on economic functions, using a "same risk, same activity, same treatment" approach while aiming for simplicity to ensure a future-proof, technology-neutral stance. However, this mitigation of regulatory arbitrage risks remains a work in progress, and many national authorities still lag in upgrading their policy frameworks and addressing regulatory fragmentation.

A string of recent failures and bankruptcies of crypto projects and intermediaries point to the financial risks stemming from, for example, risk management, governance, conflicts of interest, liquidity and maturity mismatches, high leverage, and tight financial interlinkages. These events call for action related to, among others, improving transparency and disclosure; strengthening accounting and auditing; bridging data gaps; separating economic activities carried out by centralized crypto-asset service providers (for example, custody, proprietary trading, credit provision, exchange, and clearing); creating a globally consistent and comprehensive regulatory and supervisory approach; and bolstering domestic and cross-border coordination between relevant regulators.

Some types of crypto-assets—notably global stablecoins—have the potential to attract broad public use as a means of payments, including in the DeFi ecosystem. In this context, public authorities are exploring issuing central bank digital currencies (CBDCs). Widespread adoption of crypto-assets could challenge the primacy of public money, with implications for, among other things, monetary policy and financial stability.

Some authorities have also noted the concentration, data protection, and privacy risks that large-scale payment service providers can pose, particularly the ones employing a data monetization-led business strategy. It is perceived that a CBDC, being a digital version of fiat currency, could imbue public money with the necessary digital features and enable it to provide a safer and efficient alternative to society while promoting competition and innovation. The perceived potential of CBDCs to advance financial inclusion is also of interest to some public authorities, notably the EMDEs. However, CBDCs are not a panacea for financial inclusion since key behavioral, technological, and infrastructural barriers faced by other digital payment solutions may remain in place.

Several jurisdictions and international standard-setting bodies are studying design options and developing road maps to introduce CBDCs (Kosse and Mattei 2022). The scale and pace of adoption and implications are not fully clear at this point, but the general thrust appears to position CBDCs as coexisting with other forms of money and payment mechanisms. The use of CBDCs could either be limited to regulated financial-sector players (wholesale) or open to all (retail).

Wholesale CBDCs, given their limited use, do not pose any significant policy challenges. A retail CBDC may, however, hinder bank funding and credit intermediation, reduce monetary stability, distort the level playing field, and raise financial integrity and data privacy challenges. As such, policy makers must give careful attention to various implementation options related to, for example, distribution, wallet limits, remuneration, privacy features, onboarding, and verification mechanisms.

At the time of writing, The Bahamas, the Eastern Caribbean Central Bank, and Nigeria have already launched retail CBDCs, with a few more in advanced stages: China, Ghana, and Jamaica have launched large-scale live testing. The guidance emerging from standard-setting bodies—notably, the Committee on Payments and Market Structures (CPMI) of the Bank for International Settlements—calls for striking a balanced approach. This approach would likely translate to retail CBDCs being distributed through regulated banks and payment service providers, being interoperable and coexisting with private money, and being subject to limits on transactions and restrictions on cross-border use.

Policy makers are also actively pursuing other avenues to advance the reach and efficiency of payment systems. The reforms being pursued include implementing fast payment systems, expanding access to payment systems to nonbank entrants, promoting open banking, extending hours of operations, and expanding direct access to central bank settlement services to non bank institutions. These reforms could also enable the smoother introduction of CBDCs at a later stage.

Attending to Regulatory and Supervisory Frameworks

The cross-sectoral nature of fintech has profound implications for regulatory frameworks. The growing diversity of financial service providers resulting from atomization and unbundling requires the reevaluation of the regulatory perimeter, as further examined in chapter 5 and the Regulation Note (Gispert et al. 2022).

Regulators are confronted with three questions: what to regulate, when to regulate, and how to regulate. Finance has long been intertwined with other commercial activities. Long-standing practices related to payment terms for account payables implicitly include credit extension. The terms of such credit may come under commercial conduct codes, but it is generally not part of financial sector regulation. Further, given atomization and unbundling, multiple financial and nonfinancial entities are often involved in the production of financial services. Bringing every other instance of finance and all entities involved in the production of financial services under the financial sector regulatory perimeter would not be viable in most markets. At the same time, addressing conduct-related risks might necessitate defining a wider financial sector regulatory and oversight perimeter. The potential "barbell" market outcome requires financial sector regulators to take an active role in collaboration and coordination with competition authorities to lower the barriers to entry and keep the market contestable—even when there could be natural tendencies toward market concentration in some financial services.

These regulatory challenges, in turn, have implications for supervisory frameworks. The expansion of the regulatory perimeter will have a knock-on effect on supervisory approaches and could stretch supervisory capacities. Establishing a risk-based framework to prioritize supervisory actions and calibrate supervisory intensity becomes relevant. Further, supervisors will need to marshal new skills through strategic staffing, partnerships, and industry collaborations. Strengthening and expanding data-sharing and collaboration frameworks among domestic authorities and at the international level are important. As the fintech market evolves, ensuring an orderly exit of unviable market players could become critical, necessitating the strengthening of wind-down processes and tools as well as financial sector safeguards.

Finally, in this context, the design and governance of financial infrastructures become a key policy lever to fully harness efficiency gains and safeguard competition. Several financial infrastructure components will become central to the financial services chain. Ensuring open, fair, and transparent access to these infrastructures becomes critical to provide a level playing field and allow new entrants a fair chance to compete with incumbents. Payment systems, credit reporting systems, and secured transaction registries are particularly relevant. In addition, increasing reliance on remote provision of services and data-driven processes requires new types of financial infrastructure to emerge—for example, digital ID, data-exchange hubs, and gateways to data held with governments.

Addressing the Policy Implications

In sum, the ongoing digital transformation presents a paradigm shift whose policy implications point toward the following objectives:

- *Foster beneficial innovation and competition* while managing risks.

- *Broaden the monitoring horizons and reassess regulatory perimeters* as embedding of financial services blurs the boundaries of the financial sector.

- *Be mindful of evolving policy trade-offs* as fintech adoption deepens.

- *Review regulatory, supervisory, and oversight frameworks* to ensure that they remain fit for purpose and enable the authorities to foster a safe, efficient, and inclusive financial system.

- *Anticipate market structure tendencies* and proactively shape them to foster competition and contestability in the financial sector.

- *Modernize and open up financial infrastructures* to enable competition and contestability.

- *Ensure that public money remains fit for the digital world* amid rapid advances in private money solutions.

- *Pursue strong cross-border coordination* and sharing of information and best practices, given the supranational nature of fintech.

Organization of This Publication

The chapters of the publication proceed as follows:

- *Chapter 1, Introduction,* describes the various dimensions of fintech; presents the publication's conceptual framework for examining fintech-related interactions between markets, policy, and development; and examines data on global fintech activity and trends that provide context for subsequent chapters.

- *Chapter 2, Fundamental Drivers of Fintech,* discusses the advances in two key areas—data and connectivity—that have driven digitization of a broad range of financial activities and hence new business models. It also summarizes the impacts of these economic forces on providers and consumers alike.

- *Chapter 3, Market Outcomes,* discusses how two transformative fintech innovations—digital money and digital lending—have already reshaped financial market outcomes and how various other fintech applications also affect financial infrastructures; business models; and new products, new players, and market structures in their respective markets.

- *Chapter 4, Core Policy Objectives and Evolving Trade-Offs,* examines the policy issues facing national authorities as they seek to foster the benefits of digital transformation while also addressing potential risks.

- *Chapter 5, Regulation and Supervision,* covers recent developments in fintech regulation and supervision along with key emerging issues.

- *Chapter 6, Policy Implications and Principles for Action,* concludes by summarizing the broad implications of fintech and digital transformation for financial sector policy, monetary policy, and international cooperation.

References

Boeddu, Gian and Jennifer Chien. 2022. "Financial Consumer Protection and Fintech: An Overview of New Manifestations of Consumer Risks and Emerging Regulatory Approaches." Consumer Protection technical note for *Fintech and the Future of Finance*, World Bank, Washington, DC.

Delort, Dorothee, and Jose Antonio Garcia Garcia Luna. 2022. "Innovation in Payments: Opportunities and Challenges for EMDEs." Payments technical note for *Fintech and the Future of Finance*, World Bank Group, Washington, DC.

Didier, Tatiana, Erik Feyen, Ruth Llovet Montañés, and Oya Ardic. 2022. "Global Patterns of Fintech Activity and Enabling Factors." Fintech Activity technical note for *Fintech and the Future of Finance*, World Bank, Washington, DC.

Feyen, Erik, Jon Frost, Leonardo Gambacorta, Harish Natarajan, and Matthew Saal. 2022a. "Fintech and the Digital Transformation of Financial Services: Implications for Market Structure and Public Policy." Market Structure technical note for *Fintech and the Future of Finance*, World Bank, Washington, DC.

Feyen, Erik, Jon Frost, Harish Natarajan, and Tara Rice. 2022b. "What Does Digital Money Mean for Emerging Market and Developing Economies?" Digital Money technical note for *Fintech and the Future of Finance*, World Bank, Washington, DC.

Feyen, Erik, Harish Natarajan, Guillermo Galicia Rabadan, Robert Paul Heffernan, Matthew Saal, and Arpita Sarkar. 2022c. "World Bank Group Global Market Survey: Digital Technology and the Future of Finance." Technical note for *Fintech and the Future of Finance*, World Bank, Washington, DC.

Gispert, Tatiana Alonso, Pierre-Laurent Chatain, Karl Driessen, Danilo Palermo, and Ariadne Plaitakis. 2022. "Regulation and Supervision of Fintech: Considerations for EMDE Policymakers." Regulation technical note for *Fintech and the Future of Finance*, World Bank, Washington, DC.

Kosse, Anneke, and Ilaria Mattei. 2022. "Gaining Momentum – Results of the 2021 BIS Survey on Central Bank Digital Currencies." BIS Papers No. 125, Bank for International Settlements, Basel, Switzerland.

Teima, Ghada, Ivor Istuk, Luis Maldonado, Miguel Soriano, and John Wilson. 2022. "Fintech and SME Finance: Expanding Responsible Access." SME technical note for *Fintech and the Future of Finance*, World Bank, Washington, DC.

World Bank. 2022. *World Development Report 2022: Finance for an Equitable Recovery*. Washington, DC: World Bank.

CHAPTER 1

Introduction

About Fintech and the Future of Finance

Digital transformation is reshaping the market outcomes of the financial services industry. Financial technology (fintech) supports growth and poverty alleviation by strengthening financial development, inclusion, and efficiency and by providing the financial services that are required for the digital economy to flourish. To reap these benefits, authorities will need to shape regulatory and supervisory approaches to harness these opportunities while ensuring that core policy objectives—such as stability, integrity, consumer protection, and competition—continue to be met as the digital transformation of the financial sector continues.

Digital finance has enabled providers to leapfrog legacy channels and products, particularly in emerging markets and developing economies (EMDEs). Financial markets have seen the entry of stand-alone consumer fintech firms, new business-to-business (B2B) services, and "Big Tech" firms.[1] Incumbents have also embraced technology as a strategic priority to improve their products, lower costs, and compete.

Adoption and further innovation have accelerated because of the COVID-19 pandemic, which spurred increased digitization across many sectors, including finance, as businesses and individuals adapted to social distancing and hygiene protocols and sought efficient and effective ways to connect remotely to government and business services (see appendix C). The pandemic thus reinforced what was already a clear trend of rapid advances in technology reshaping the economic and financial landscape globally (IMF and World Bank 2019; Pazarbasioglu et al. 2020).

This publication responds to increasing demand from policy makers for guidance as their financial sectors transform. It explores how fintech is reshaping the structure of financial services, the implications of fintech in key product areas and for different customer segments, and potential regulatory responses. Two key questions guided these explorations:

- *What are the most important likely market outcomes* in terms of (a) types of financial services providers; (b) types of business models, products, and services; (c) market structure; and (d) infrastructures in the financial sector in EMDEs over the next five to 10 years?

- *What policy responses might shape or change these outcomes* in support of policy objectives and priorities, given EMDE conditions and constraints?

This publication is intended as a nonexhaustive, nontechnical narrative of the most salient developments and policy issues. It is aimed at senior policy makers and practitioners, and it draws from the set of eight technical notes (box 1.1) that

---

BOX 1.1

Fintech and the Future of Finance Technical Notes

Data Trends and Market Perceptions

1. "Global Patterns of Fintech Activity and Enabling Factors" (Fintech Activity Note) by Tatiana Didier, Erik Feyen, Ruth Llovet Montañés, and Oya Ardic
2. "World Bank Group Global Market Survey: Digital Technology and the Future of Finance" (Fintech Market Participants Survey) by Erik Feyen, Harish Natarajan, Robert Paul Heffernan, Matthew Saal, Arpita Sarkar, and Guillermo Galicia Rabadan

Policy Issues

3. "Fintech and the Digital Transformation of Financial Services: Implications for Market Structure and Public Policy" (Market Structure Note) by Erik Feyen, Jon Frost, Leonardo Gambacorta, Harish Natarajan, and Matthew Saal
4. "Regulation and Supervision of Fintech: Considerations for EMDE Policymakers" (Regulation Note) by Tatiana Alonso Gispert, Pierre-Laurent Chatain, Karl Driessen, Danilo Palermo, and Ariadne Plaitakis, with contributions from Ana M. Carvajal and Matei Dohotaru
5. "Financial Consumer Protection and Fintech: An Overview of New Manifestations of Consumer Risks and Emerging Regulatory Approaches" (Consumer Protection Note) by Gian Boeddu and Jennifer Chien

Specific Fintech Products

6. "Innovation in Payments: Opportunities and Challenges for EMDEs" (Payments Note) by Dorothee Delort and Jose Antonio Garcia Garcia Luna
7. "Fintech and SME Finance: Expanding Responsible Access" (SME Note) by Ghada Teima, Ivor Istuk, Luis Maldonado, Miguel Soriano, and John Wilson
8. "What Does Digital Money Mean for Emerging Market and Developing Economies?" (Digital Money Note) by Erik Feyen, Jon Frost, Harish Natarajan, and Tara Rice

make up the overall report; these notes contain in-depth descriptions of developments, trends, and policy recommendations. Appendix B contains all the executive summaries of the technical notes.

This publication is part of an ongoing research, advisory, and investment agenda; it builds on prior research and work in this space by practitioners from the World Bank Group and other institutions and firms. Prior work has included the Bali Fintech Agenda; advisory and policy work with governments, regulators, and standard-setting bodies; World Bank–International Monetary Fund (IMF) Financial Sector Assessment Program (FSAP) analyses of fintech developments; and the accumulated experience of the International Finance Corporation (IFC) as a pioneer investor in emerging markets' fintech. This publication leverages a unique data set of fintech adoption metrics; a global survey of banks, multilateral financial institutions, nonbank financial institutions, fintech companies, and others; and the experience of global fintech, finance, and regulatory experts.

The World Bank continues to assess fintech developments and advise governments and central banks on fintech issues in coordination with the IMF, the Financial Stability Board (FSB), the Committee on Payments and Market Infrastructures, the Group of Twenty (G-20), the Global Partnership for Financial Inclusion, and other relevant organizations. IFC is complementing its investment in fintech firms and the digital transformation of traditional financial institutions with research and thought leadership on the private sector growth and investment opportunities emerging from fintech adoption, including in areas such as small and medium enterprise (SME) finance and embedded finance.

Conceptual Framework

This publication is framed around the development of and interactions between four key factors that are relevant for fintech: fundamental fintech developments or drivers; market outcomes; core policy objectives; and policy making (figure 1.1). This conceptual framework captures the implications of fintech and the digital transformation under way in financial services for (a) market outcomes (summarized in the top portion of figure 1.1), and (b) policy making (in the bottom portion)—and how these two aspects interact. The impact of fintech drivers on market outcomes typically requires a policy response to ensure alignment with policy objectives, which in turn shapes market outcomes, producing a feedback loop.

Within this framework, fundamental technology developments shape market outcomes. Advances in computation and connectivity have produced massive amounts of data and alleviated transaction costs as well as frictions associated with financial services provision. These technological factors—combined with scale and scope economies and network effects—have profoundly transformed financial sector business models, products, infrastructures, market players, and market structures. These technological innovations are ultimately not purely exogenous, because innovators respond to market conditions and create the next generation of technologies.

Another key factor involves the core policy objectives—such as financial inclusion, efficiency, and stability—that drive the formulation of regulatory and supervisory frameworks. This publication distinguishes long-standing policy objectives, but these too are not immutable. For example, financial inclusion and consumer data protection have emerged relatively recently as policy objectives

FIGURE 1.1 Conceptual Framework for Fintech: Interactions between Markets, Policy, and Development

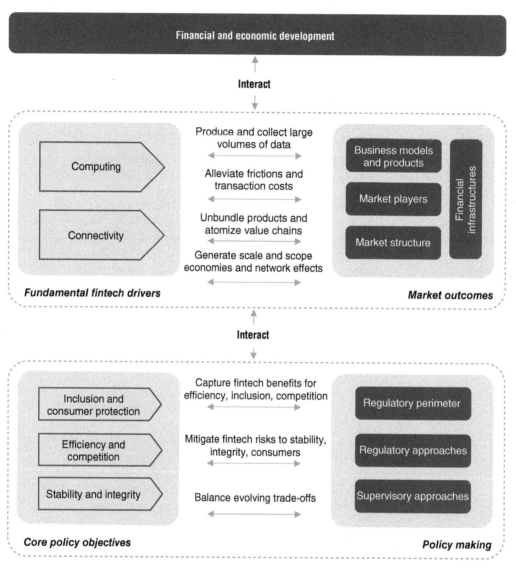

Source: Original elaboration for this publication.

in their own right. Policy makers' objective regarding financial innovation is to capture the main benefits of fintech while mitigating associated risks. Doing this requires balancing trade-offs that continuously evolve as the sector's digital transformation progresses and market outcomes change.

These dynamics also depend on a country's stage of fintech development. At lower levels of fintech development, the range of services, scale, and penetration is still limited. This stage calls for policy makers' willingness to support innovation and to provide basic legal and regulatory clarity. Addressing data gaps that prevent effective monitoring of risks, safeguarding the most vulnerable customers, and ensuring that financial integrity objectives are met are key priorities because risks to financial stability, fair competition, and overall consumer and investor protection are still relatively low. However, as scale, complexity, interconnectedness, and possible concentration increase, policy makers must increase their focus on safeguarding financial stability, data protection, and fair competition. This enhanced focus requires that legal, regulatory, and supervisory frameworks—as well as technology and financial infrastructures—be reviewed and strengthened to support the development of a flourishing fintech ecosystem that remains consistent with policy objectives.

Fintech: What It Is and Why It Matters

Fintech can be defined in various ways. The Bali Fintech Agenda, the FSB, and others broadly define fintech as "advances in technology that have the potential to transform the provision of financial services spurring the development of new business models, applications, processes, and products" (IMF and World Bank 2019).[2] The accompanying technical notes (summarized in appendix B) address specific technologies, where relevant. The overall focus here, however, is on the market trends and regulatory implications of the digital transformation of finance in the context of rapidly digitizing economies, rather than on specific technologies that may have currency today but may be superseded tomorrow. For that reason, this publication starts its analysis with the key drivers of change on the technology side and links these to the underlying economics of financial intermediation: the economic frictions that gave rise to intermediaries as well as the economic forces that shaped their scope and scale.

Technology can lower costs and increase the speed, transparency, security, and availability of more tailored financial services. Digitization can reduce frictions in each step along the financial service life cycle, from opening an account to conducting customer due diligence; authenticating transactions; and automating other, product-specific processes such as assessing creditworthiness. Fintech is therefore characterized by low marginal costs per account or transaction and scale efficiencies. Fintech can also enhance transparency and reduce information asymmetries, since digital processes generate a data trail, which can be used to better understand consumers, improve products, manage risks, and promote regulatory compliance.

History and Context

The use of technology in finance has a long history. In fact, because finance involves high-value activities, there has always been an incentive to use the latest technology—whether it was the finest scale to weigh gold pieces or the fastest communication methods of the day, from Rothschild's carrier pigeons to Reuter's telegraph. Digital technology made its way into finance as the second major application of electronic computers after the military.

The first wave of financial technology in the 1950s to 1970s saw mainframe computer systems become part of the fabric of the back office, moving gradually to the middle and front offices of most large financial institutions. The late 1960s through the 1980s saw the emergence of digital technology companies dedicated to serving financial institutions, including core banking system providers like

Fidelity National Information Services (FIS) and Fiserv as well as payments networks like Mastercard and the Society for Worldwide Interbank Financial Telecommunications (SWIFT).

The current wave of fintech innovation is marked by increasingly direct interaction between technology companies and their customers as these companies become the providers of financial services themselves. This wave leverages the increasingly sophisticated technology that is in the hands of increasingly sophisticated customers, along with innovations in business models, to disaggregate services and offer new reconfigurations of products directly to individuals and business users.

This process has disrupted the market in terms of the pace of technological advances, who is providing financial services, and how consumers use those services and interact with providers. This effect is evident, for example, in the statistics on global uptake of mobile money accounts and increases in mobile money transactions (figure 1.2). The World Bank's Global Findex survey shows that mobile money operators added more than twice as many accounts as banks in Sub-Saharan Africa from 2014 to 2017, becoming the key drivers of increased financial access (Demirgüç-Kunt et al. 2022). A significant majority (92 percent) of respondents to the Fintech Market Participants Survey indicated that fintech and digital transformation is a strategic priority at the board level of their organizations (Feyen et al. 2022).[3]

Innovation in Fintech Payment and Lending

Innovation has taken hold across different areas of financial services to different degrees. However, payments have been at the forefront. Digital payments have

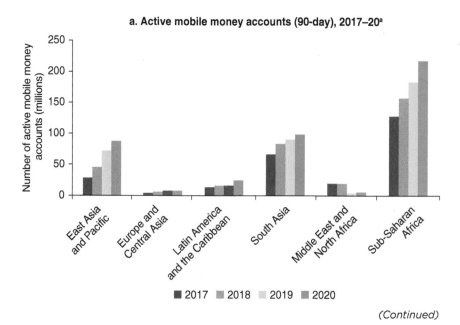

FIGURE 1.2 **Growth in Mobile Money Accounts and Transactions, 2017–20**

a. Active mobile money accounts (90-day), 2017–20[a]

■ 2017 ▨ 2018 ▨ 2019 ■ 2020

(Continued)

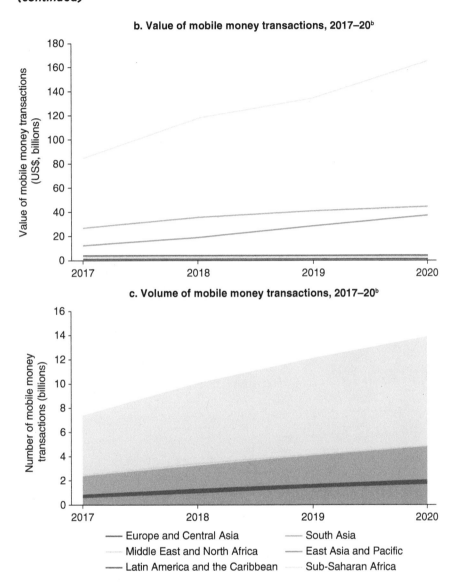

b. Value of mobile money transactions, 2017–20[b]

c. Volume of mobile money transactions, 2017–20[b]

Source: "Global Metrics," Global System for Mobile Communications Association (GSMA) Mobile Money Metrics database (https://www.gsma.com/mobilemoneymetrics/#global).
a. Data are as of the end of December in each year.
b. Data are the sum of quarterly data for each year.

become important in all regions and almost all countries, as illustrated by map 1.1, which shows the fintech digital payments and credit indexes developed in the Fintech Activity Note for this publication (Didier et al. 2022). In some markets, such as Bangladesh, China, and Kenya, significant portions of payments volume and value are processed through nonbank mobile wallets. In other markets, bank account and card-based systems (most of which link to underlying bank accounts) dominate.

Fintech lending lags payments but is becoming significant (map 1.1, panel b). The Fintech Activity Note index shows Australia, China, Europe, and the United States leading in fintech lending, but important levels of activity are emerging in other parts of Asia as well as in Africa and Latin America (Didier et al. 2022). The Bank for International Settlements (BIS) and the Cambridge Centre for Alternative Finance (CCAF) estimated that global fintech lending had reached

MAP 1.1 **Global Use of Digital Payments and Fintech Credit**

a. Digital payments (index)

b. Fintech credit (index)

Source: Didier et al. 2022.

US$125 billion, and Big Tech lending US$637 billion, in 2020 (Cornelli et al. 2020), as shown in figure 1.3, panel a.

Although the total of these two forms of "alternative credit" was estimated to be less than 2 percent in most of the major fintech markets (figure 1.3, panel b), one recent industry analysis projects global fintech lending to rise to US$4.9 trillion by 2030 (AMR 2021). Accordingly, alternative credit could soon be a significant portion of credit creation. To the extent that alternative credit grows in part at the expense of traditional credit providers, the relative shift in market share and credit emission to providers outside the traditional regulated banking system would accelerate.

Fintech Investment Trends

The range of players in financial services is increasing rapidly, with increasing sums invested into nonbank fintech players. The total value of fintech investments worldwide rose from under US$10 billion per year before 2013 to US$215 billion in 2019 before falling back to "only" US$122 billion in 2020.[4] By the first half of 2021, fintech investments had already reached US$98 billion (figure 1.4).

Although high-income markets are the largest recipients of funding, EMDEs are also showing significant levels of fintech investment (map 1.2).

FIGURE 1.3 Global Growth in Big Tech Credit Relative to Fintech Credit

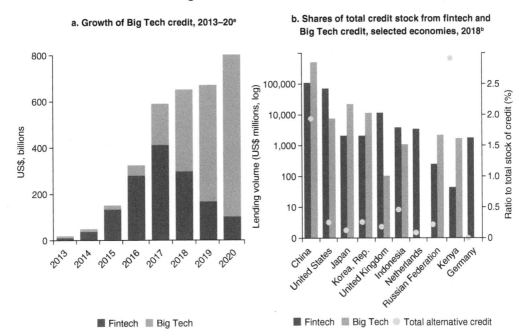

a. Growth of Big Tech credit, 2013–20[a]

b. Shares of total credit stock from fintech and Big Tech credit, selected economies, 2018[b]

Source: Cornelli et al. 2020; updated estimates.
Note: "Fintech" refers to advanced technologies that could transform provision of financial services. "Big Tech" encompasses large companies whose primary activity is in digital services and that have large customer bases for those services. Data not available for Big Tech for Germany and the Netherlands.
a. Credit data include estimates.
b. Lending volume data are from 2019. The data on total stocks of domestic credit, provided by the financial sector, are from 2018. The yellow dots designate the ratio of "total alternative credit" (the sum of fintech and Big Tech credit) to the economy's total stock of credit, as measured in the right y-axis.

FIGURE 1.4 **Growth in Fintech Investments over the Past Decade**

a. Global fintech investments, 2010–21

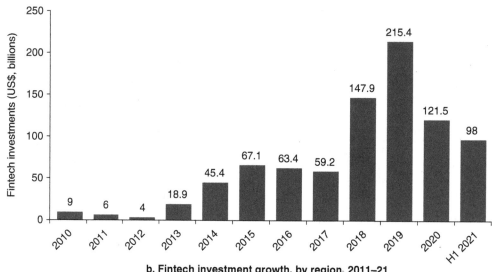

b. Fintech investment growth, by region, 2011–21

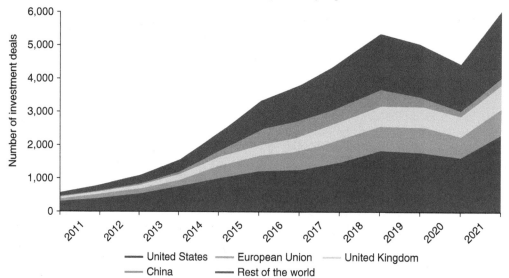

Sources: Statista Research Department data, 2022 (https://www.statista.com/statistics/719385/investments-into-fintech-companies-globally/); Cornelli et al. 2021.
Note: H1 = first half.

Policy Implications

These maps show that fintech and digital transformation are relevant across market types. Although high-income markets tend to show more activity, financial innovation has had far-reaching impacts in many EMDEs. As a result, every regulator concerned with financial stability, financial inclusion, financial system integrity and efficiency, competition, consumer protection, or simply with tracking how

MAP 1.2 Equity Investments in Fintech Companies

Source: Didier et al. 2022.

the macroeconomic levers over money supply and credit are changing has taken note of the disruptive changes that fintech is bringing to the financial system and the broader economy.

Notes

1. For further explanation of "Big Tech," see the glossary following the appendixes.
2. For further definition of the Bali Fintech Agenda, fintech, and other related terms, see the glossary following the appendixes.
3. This survey was conducted from May 2020 to January 2021. The respondents included 330 market participants from 109 countries, representing traditional banks, payments and remittance service providers, fintech firms, insurance companies, nonbanking companies, technology companies, telecommunications companies, industry associations, and other financial market players. Given the number of respondents, countries, and subsectors, the survey may not be fully representative of every country and institution type. For more information, see Feyen et al. (2022) or the summary of the work in appendix B.
4. "Total value of investments into fintech companies worldwide from 2010 to 2021," Statista Research Department data, https://www.statista.com /statistics/719385/investments-into-fintech-companies-globally/.

References

AMR (Allied Market Research). 2021. "FinTech Lending Market to Reach $4,957.16 Billion, Globally, by 2030 at 27.4% CAGR." PRNewswire news release, November 15.

Cornelli, Giulio, Sebastian Doerr, Lavinia Franco, and Jon Frost. 2021. "Funding for Fintechs: Patterns and Drivers." *BIS Quarterly Review* (September 2021): 31–43.

Cornelli, Giulio, Jon Frost, Leonardo Gambacorta, Raghavendra Rau, Robert Wardrop, and Tania Ziegler. 2020. "Fintech and Big Tech Credit: A New Database." Working Paper No. 887, Bank for International Settlements, Basel, Switzerland.

Demirgüç-Kunt, Asli, Leora Klapper, Dorothe Singer, and Saniya Ansar. 2022. *The Global Findex Database 2021: Financial Inclusion, Digital Payments, and Resilience in the Age of COVID-19.* Washington, DC: World Bank.

Didier, Tatiana, Erik Feyen, Ruth Llovet Montañés, and Oya Ardic. 2022. "Global Patterns of Fintech Activity and Enabling Factors." Fintech Activity technical note for *Fintech and the Future of Finance*, World Bank, Washington, DC.

Feyen, Erik, Harish Natarajan, Robert Paul Heffernan, Matthew Saal, Arpita Sarkar, and Guillermo Galicia Rabadan. 2022. "World Bank Group Global Market Survey: Digital Technology and the Future of Finance." Fintech Market Participants Survey report for *Fintech and the Future of Finance*, World Bank, Washington, DC.

IMF (International Monetary Fund) and World Bank. 2019. "Fintech: The Experience So Far." Policy Paper No. 2019/024, IMF and World Bank, Washington, DC.

Pazarbasioglu, Ceyla, Alfonso Garcia Mora, Mahesh Uttamchandani, Harish Natarajan, Erik Feyen, and Mathew Saal. 2020. "Digital Financial Services." Report, World Bank, Washington, DC.

CHAPTER 2

Fundamental Drivers of Fintech

Key Technologies: Connectivity and Computing Power

Digital technology is reshaping financial services by eliminating many of the frictions that drove earlier integrated business models through advances in two key areas: connectivity and computing power. The internet and mobile technology have increased connectivity among consumers, financial services providers, and a range of intermediate service providers and customer interfaces.[1] Ubiquitous connectivity has eliminated barriers and reduced costs for information transfer and remote interactions. In emerging markets and developing economies (EMDEs), where barriers to financial access and costs of services have been high, mobile connectivity has enabled markets to leapfrog past the constraints of fixed line and bank branch infrastructure. Basic access through at least a feature phone is available to billions of individuals across markets. Low-cost computing and data storage put processing power such as smartphones at the end of each of those ubiquitous connection points, enabling complex transactions and services; generating vast amounts of data; and facilitating the efficient processing, storage, and analysis of that data.

The resulting digitization of a broad range of activities, including finance, is creating massive volumes of data that can be leveraged to broaden and deepen financial services and better manage risk. A variety of sources generate these data, including the location and usage data from mobile phones, the contact information from social networks, the delivery information from logistics companies, and the sales data from retail outlets and payments networks. Such data are being used in a wide range of traditional financial services and new types of businesses to improve credit analysis, process efficiency, risk management, product design, customer service, and other areas. Advances in analytics—including artificial intelligence—enable automation, process improvements, and new approaches to risk management.

Together, ubiquitous connectivity and scalable computing and data storage enable the development of cloud-based computing and data storage infrastructure. The result is an ability to increase processing efficiency, to gather and analyze large data sets, to obtain infrastructure on demand, and to reduce the fixed cost barrier to entry in financial services and other industries. Combined with software as a service (SaaS)[2] and cloud-based analytics offerings, niche-focused financial services can be viable at low volumes and can scale as they grow their customer base. Most fintech start-ups use cloud-based services to keep their own infrastructure cost low and leverage the scalable and data analytics capabilities of the large cloud providers. At the same time, digitization of processes creates more digitally available data, and scalable infrastructure allows reams of data to be stored and analyzed.

Another result of these technology advances has been the emergence of platform-based business models in e-commerce and social media markets. These businesses leverage the connectivity of individuals and businesses as well as the ability to quickly and easily collaborate, discover counterparties, and package and deliver a range of digital and physical goods and services. Such business models benefit from strong network effects. Adding users on one side of a platform market (ride-hailing drivers, for example) creates more value to users on the other side (riders). The platform becomes more attractive on the first side (drivers), attracting even more users. In addition to the presence of a diverse set of counterparties, more participation allows the platform to mine more data about users, behaviors, and preferences; to create better matches; or to better tailor its own products and services. A positive growth spiral can result in a "winner-takes-all" type of outcome, where all market participants want to benefit from the network effects of being on the same platform.

Platform business models that aggregate and link buyers and sellers are also being adopted for price comparison, distribution, and origination of financial products like lending, investment, and insurance—in some cases, by the same real-sector platforms discussed. The platform operators are embedding financial services to improve the experience of their different customer constituencies. For example, ride-hailing services in many countries provide payment services to improve the safety and efficiency of the payment process for both drivers and riders, and they also seek to facilitate drivers' access to insurance and to credit to purchase and maintain their vehicles.

Impact of Technology

The technological advances described have affected every industry, and their impacts on financial services have been particularly profound. Many aspects of finance were already digitized behind the scenes; most of the value of global payment flows, for example, were already executed through computer-to-computer transactions. This wave of technology has resulted in the unbundling of financial products, the reconfiguration of the value chains that produce and deliver financial products and services, and the entry of new providers.

The initial impacts were disaggregation and atomization at the product level and the potential for a much more fragmented financial services sector at the provider level. However, as explained in the following section, "Impact of Economic Forces: Scale Economies, Frictions, and Rebundling," traditional economic forces that shape industry structure—such as economies of scale and scope, search costs, and transaction frictions—remain relevant, albeit in new forms. These forces counterbalance the tendency toward fragmentation; they are, in fact, driving a rebundling of services and potential acceleration of sector concentration.

Unbundling and Reconfiguration of Value Chains

The application of technological advances to producing financial services alleviates fixed-cost constraints as well as frictions related to transaction costs and incomplete information. Increased connectivity and cloud-based computing allow new entrants to reach customers without investment in traditional branch and data center infrastructure. Connectivity and vast amounts of user data can increase transparency and trust while also improving credit assessment, thereby reducing the risk cost of lending.

The potential to transfer data between different providers at different points in the production of a financial service enables disaggregation and reconfiguration of value chains. Vertical integration of activities within a single firm is a means of avoiding the transaction costs of working across multiple suppliers and producers to assemble product through market-mediated exchanges of goods or services (Coase 1937; Williamson 1975). Digital connectivity and rich data sharing reduce or eliminate many of the transaction and monitoring costs of market-mediated exchanges, obviating the need for vertical integration.

A producer can use outsourcing and partnership arrangements to unbundle products and incorporate atomized solutions from specialist providers of component products, subprocesses, or functions. Financial institutions increasingly use specialist providers for customer onboarding; verification and Know Your Customer (KYC) procedures; credit scoring; loan processing; and other services provided under their own brands. These institutions partner with consumer-facing fintech firms and other new brands where they do not have their own products. Interoperable payment systems, application programming interfaces (APIs), and open-banking protocols have made it even easier to knit together services from different providers. In this way, data, analytics, and automation can result in market demand being met more fully—that is, they can create more complete markets—by enabling the tailoring of products and services to the needs of well-defined customer segments or even each individual consumer.

Technology developments, accompanied by enabling regulatory frameworks, have allowed for the separation of payment services from the maintenance of accounts. Specifically, e-money created a payment service distinct from a bank account, hence enabling nonbank entities to enter the payment services business. And "open banking" is enabling third-party applications to initiate payment transactions without even having to maintain any account, taking unbundling even further. These advances reduce the barriers to entry for new providers, including providers of new platform-based business models,[3] and enable closer integration between financial services and real-sector economic interactions (embedded finance). The ongoing development of decentralized finance (DeFi) takes this to an extreme by not requiring an account-holding institution for transaction processing or other functions.

As a result, it is increasingly easy for customers to engage in horizontal unbundling by choosing different providers of their preferred sets of services. For example, consumers may have their salaries deposited to bank accounts; automatically transfer portions for day-to-day spending to neobanks (companies offering bank-like services)[4] that offer cards with attractive budget tracking features; use a specialist remittance app for foreign transfers; and invest via one or more other providers, from peer-to-peer (P2P) lending to social stock-picking apps. Internet connectivity reduces the cost of searching for preferred products and the barriers to moving funds between them. The ease of transferring between accounts and providers allows customers to re-create the full set of an integrated financial services provider on their smartphone screens.

New Entrants

Digital innovation has reduced cost barriers, allowing the entry of more new players. New entrants do not require investment in physical access points such as branches, automated teller machines (ATMs), or agents. Although "phygital" combinations of digital and physical infrastructure continue to be needed to serve customers (even crypto-assets users were offered bitcoin ATMs), the increased interoperability and ease of outsourcing arrangements described earlier enable providers without physical networks to partner with others to offer those services, where required. Physical networks require scale and capillarity, but a few agent, branch, and ATM networks can serve a market without every provider creating and maintaining one.

The current wave of fintech innovation is marked by the entry of start-ups (fintech firms), on the one hand, and large incumbent technology companies (Big Tech firms) on the other hand. The former are often well resourced given active venture capital interest, but they lack the benefit of an existing customer base and often employ aggressive approaches to take market share from incumbents on specific products. Firms in the latter category have the advantage of existing customer bases and revenue streams, which they can leverage to scale rapidly and integrate financial services into existing products and services. Different types of entrants can have very different implications for market structure—with, in turn, different implications for financial regulation, competition, and consumer protection policies.

Niche providers can offer tailored products and services and find an interested customer base. Although they must still develop a trusted reputation, the elimination of many fixed costs and a reduction in variable and switching costs make it economically viable for a low-cost provider to enter the market. However, risks and economic forces are more stubborn than costs. Credit, liquidity, market, and operational risks can be reduced or transferred but not eliminated completely. The attack surface for cybercriminals has become larger because interconnectivity and the disaggregation of services introduce more links to each product chain and user interface.

Respondents to the Fintech Market Participants Survey conducted for this work were asked whether, in the next five years (by approximately 2025), they expect retail and small and medium enterprise (SME) customers to have a single core financial relationship or to use multiple providers with no core relationship (Feyen et al. 2022). Of the respondents, 36 percent expect customers to use multiple providers with no core relationship, and 16 percent expect that customers will have a core relationship with a marketplace or platform provider (figure 2.1).

Impact of Economic Forces: Scale Economies, Frictions, and Rebundling

Amid the entry of new niche players and shifts in business models, economies of scale and scope remain relevant. The minimum scale for efficient service delivery is now lower for financial service providers that use variable infrastructure services like cloud computing. This, however, simply shifts the scale effects to the new infrastructure providers; as such, scale remains highly relevant in areas of cloud computing, data processing, and software platforms. In fact, new forms of scale economies have emerged in connectivity (network effects) and all aspects of data provision and services alongside conventional economies of scale in capital, including reputation or "trust capital." A provider's customer acquisition and funding costs also create economies of scope: a niche provider that has a cost of customer acquisition can only amortize that cost

FIGURE 2.1 Expectations Regarding Customer Relationships with Financial Service Providers

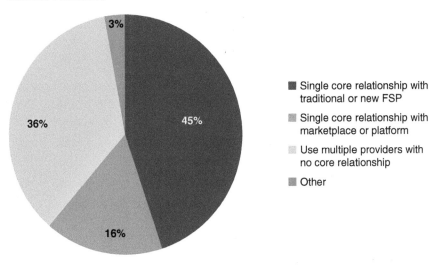

Source: Feyen et al. 2022.
Note: The chart shows the distribution of responses to a question on evolving consumer needs and behavior in the Fintech Market Participants Survey, conducted May 2020 to January 2021, of 330 fintech market participants from 109 countries. Respondents represented traditional banks, payments and remittance service providers, fintech firms, insurance companies, nonbanking companies, technology companies, telecommunications companies, industry associations, and other financial market players. For more information, see the survey report (Feyen et al. 2022) or the summary in appendix B. FSP = financial service provider.

across a limited product set, whereas adding additional products can leverage the existing customer base with lower acquisition costs.

Consumers and other users can experience frictions in the unbundled financial services marketplace. For many consumers, there is a cost to the time, effort, and potential confusion of searching for and assembling fragmented services from unbundled providers as well as potentially switching providers. Even as operational frictions of moving funds between providers have been reduced, there are still transaction costs involved. Consumer usage frictions related to finding the right solutions and managing funds across multiple providers remain a barrier to adoption; simplicity and convenience have significant value. Individuals and businesses may prefer to work with a single platform or provider that offers an integrated suite of financial products and services, even if each individual product may be less well designed, or marginally more expensive, than those of alternative niche providers. These frictions limit the degree of product atomization, value chain disaggregation, and provider diversity that the market will bear.

The combination of scale and scope economies on the provider side, and frictions on the customer side, confer advantages on providers with larger customer bases or more diversified product sets. Scale effects, alongside economies of scope and consumer convenience factors, encourage rebundling. Incumbent multiproduct banks and insurers have some of these scale and scope advantages—if they can improve customer experiences and immediacy. Fintech firms are merging or obtaining banking licenses to broaden their product sets.

This rebundling is not limited to combining financial services with other financial services; increasingly, financial services are being embedded in nonfinancial activities. Technology-enabled atomization and unbundling of accounts from other services has allowed those services, especially payments, to be conducted through applications and service providers separate from the account-holding institutions. These atomized payments services are being embedded into nonfinancial services, particularly activities conducted through digital platforms. Thus, for example, many ride-hailing services embed a wallet to seamlessly integrate payment into the ride experience. Embedding payments, credit, insurance, and investment into ride-hailing, e-commerce, logistics, social media, gaming, and other platforms has enabled Big Tech firms and others to make deep inroads into financial services.

Notes

1. Cisco (2020) predicts that more than 70 percent of the global population will have mobile connectivity by 2023 and that the number of network-connected devices will be three times the population. Fixed broadband speed is expected to almost double, from 60 megabits per second (Mbps) in 2020 to 110 Mbps in 2023, with 90 percent of connections faster than 10 Mbps.

2. SaaS, facilitated by cloud computing, refers to a software licensing and delivery model whereby centrally hosted software is licensed on a subscription basis, often via a web browser.

3. Open banking enables development of marketplace and platform business models wherein an entity can help customers to seamlessly subscribe to different services from different providers and also enables development of niche

back-end service providers who offer banking as a service (BaaS), providing the underlying building blocks—such as maintenance of a bank account or interfaces with a payment system—that others can use to develop customer-facing products and services, such as BaaS.

4. For further definition of neobanks, see the glossary following the appendixes.

References

Cisco. 2020. "Annual Internet Report (2018–2023)." White paper, Cisco Systems, San Jose, CA.

Coase, Ronald H. 1937. "The Nature of the Firm." *Economica* 4 (16): 386–405.

Feyen, Erik, Harish Natarajan, Robert Paul Heffernan, Matthew Saal, Arpita Sarkar, and Guillermo Galicia Rabadan. 2022. "World Bank Group Global Market Survey: Digital Technology and the Future of Finance." Fintech Market Participants Survey report for *Fintech and the Future of Finance*, World Bank, Washington, DC.

Williamson, Oliver E. 1975. *Markets and Hierarchies: Analysis and Antitrust Implications*. New York: Free Press.

CHAPTER 3

Market Outcomes

Impacts across the Four Dimensions of Market Outcomes

The conceptual framework shown in chapter 1 specified four dimensions of fintech's market outcomes: business models and products, market players, market structure, and financial infrastructures. Two types of transformative fintech innovations—digital payments and digital lending—are reshaping all of these four dimensions, and certain policy issues have emerged as a result.

Digital Payments

Globally, an estimated 770 billion digital payments were made in 2020 (Capgemini Research Institute 2021). Mobile money transactions alone numbered 41 billion, representing a total transaction value of US$767 billion across 300 million active mobile money accounts (GSMA 2020). Sub-Saharan Africa accounted for the bulk of mobile money transactions in 2020—27.4 billion transactions, amounting to US$490 billion across 159 million active mobile money accounts (GSMA 2021b). The volume of digital payments is growing at around 11 percent a year globally and at much higher rates in emerging markets and developing economies (EMDEs) (Capgemini 2020).

E-money issued by nonbanks, such as mobile network operators, leveraged the connectivity boom and has enabled millions of users to store value and make transactions from their phones, most notably in Sub-Saharan Africa. As users increasingly shift to smartphone use from basic phones, app-based payments can replace Unstructured Supplementary Service Data (USSD) interfaces, offering enhanced functionality (including linkage to bank accounts), speed, and convenience while also generating rich data that can be used for further services.[1]

A next generation of digital money is emerging in the form of crypto-assets and central bank digital currencies (CBDCs). Many EMDEs are looking into issuing CBDCs, in part to support the digital economy, improve payments efficiency, and promote financial inclusion. CBDCs, however, share many of the same challenges as traditional approaches to reaching and serving unbanked customers and, as such, are not a panacea for these policy objectives. Further, in addition to the proven models of e-money and agent-based basic banking models, new developments like faster payment systems, quick response (QR) codes, and open banking could provide alternative pathways.

In light of their scale, mobile money networks raise policy issues related to competition and how authorities would deal with the failure of a large, systemically important nonbank e-money issuer. Depending on how it is implemented, a CBDC may reduce bank deposits and credit intermediation and may distort the playing field on which banks and private payment service providers compete. In EMDEs, foreign CBDCs could displace local currencies and erode monetary sovereignty.

Figure 3.1 summarizes how the ongoing digital transformation of money and payments is reshaping financial market outcomes in each of the four dimensions.

Digital Lending

Providing credit through digital channels and using data-driven underwriting and risk management have been important fintech applications. The flow of digital credit was estimated at almost US$800 billion globally in 2020, with Big Tech lending platforms representing 70 percent of this lending volume (Cornelli et al. 2020; Cornelli et al. 2021).

Peer-to-peer (P2P) lending, an early alternative credit innovation, was as much a regulatory arbitrage to gather nondeposit funding as it was a means to leverage alternative data (the "wisdom of the crowd") for underwriting. Digital lenders use enhanced reach and data analytics to increase access to finance to individuals and small and medium enterprises (SMEs) that had been previously excluded for lack of proximity to a branch or lack of credit history. Embedded finance providers ranging from e-commerce and logistics platforms to consumer goods distribution networks can leverage transactional data on orders, inventory, sales, or receivables to provide working capital.

However, the wide range of alternative credit providers raises policy issues over how to treat nonbank lenders—such as whether lending is a regulated activity per se or should only be regulated in the context of protecting depositors or investors. It also raises issues regarding consumer protection of the borrower (for example, usury limits and fair disclosure) and credit information sharing with and by nonbank lenders. New technologies and data-based lending also raise policy issues concerning algorithmic bias, digital exclusion, and data privacy. In addition, the remote nature of many of these products raises challenges for Know Your Customer (KYC) practices, gauging of product appropriateness, and consumer disclosures and education. Finally, significant growth of digital lending could have implications for monetary policy management if alternative lenders are less directly affected by standard policy levers.

Figure 3.2 summarizes how the ongoing digital transformation of lending is reshaping the four dimensions of market outcomes.

FIGURE 3.1 **Market Outcomes of Digital Money and Payments, by Dimension**

Business models and products

- E-money spawned a range of new products, from wallets to mobile lending applications (discussed in the "Digital Lending" section). CBDCs will further accelerate payments product innovation including cross-border application.
- Third-party payment initiation with payment services enabling a nonbank entity to package payment services as part of a broader range of financial and nonfinancial services.
- Lower the cost of payment services to the point where payment is no longer a profit center but an enabler for other services.

Market players

- Nonfinancial companies such as telcos, Big Tech platforms, and NBFIs such as PSPs have become significant players in e-money issuance and wallet operation. Increased use of e-money and third-party payment initiation has created opportunities for a broad range of payment acceptance facilitators.
- Organizers of distributed ledgers and exchanges providing on- and off-ramps for crypto-assets have become important players in digital money.

Market structure

- New entry reduces market power of existing network oligopolies.
- Network effects lead to concentration.
- Because of network effects and early-mover advantages, e-money has emerged as a monopoly or duopoly in many markets. In others, a multiplicity of wallet providers have entered.
- Crypto-assets could in principle offer numerous competing media of exchange and stores of value but, here too, network effects have tended to result in a few prominent players.

Financial infrastructure

- Digital money may supplant existing payment system infrastructures with private ledgers processing payments internally (e-money issuers) or public distributed ledgers.
- Crypto-assets can bypass existing payment infrastructures but have in practice created a new layer of exchange infrastructure; whether that is a permanent feature or a transitory phase remains to be seen.
- A basic feature phone can replace the need to access a bank branch or traditional payment account or a POS terminal. As broadly available as that may be, a complete shift to digital payments could exclude those lacking network connectivity, or, in the case of more complex products, those lacking a smartphone.
- Fast initiation of payments using QR codes and APIs, and faster and round-the-clock processing of payments, are creating new payment products for making and receiving payments in person, remotely, and across borders.

Source: Original elaboration for this publication.
Note: API = application programming interface; CBDC = central bank digital currency; NBFI = nonbank financial institution; POS = point-of-service; PSP = payment service provider; QR = quick response; telcos = telecommunications companies.

Impacts of Other Fintech Applications

Beyond these two illustrative examples—of digital payments and digital lending—other applications of fintech also affect the financial infrastructure, business models and products, market players, and market structures in their respective markets. Among them is insurtech: technological innovations that improve the efficiency of the insurance industry. Although insurtech is now a smaller market than digital payments and credit, it too is shifting the market structure of producers, brokers, and agents—as well as how policies are underwritten and claims serviced—using data and Internet of Things connectivity.

In addition, digital wealth management and investment applications have broadened access to products and encouraged more active participation by retail

FIGURE 3.2 Market Outcomes of Digital Lending, by Dimension

Business models and products
• Peer-to-peer lending platforms • Mobile phone lending apps • Buy-now-pay-later (BNPL) products • Invoice exchange and finance • Stand-alone bank microloan products • Mobile network credit to mobile money agents and merchants • Merchant working capital loans via e-commerce platforms • B2B marketplace accounts receivable finance

Market players
• Fintech lenders, including lenders, peer-to-peer, platforms, digital NBFIs, and mobile phone microlenders • Regulated traditional lenders digitizing their channels and products • Big Tech embedded finance, including mobile network credit to agents, and e-commerce merchant loans • Supply chain participants offering credit in the order-inventory process • Lending-as-a-Service (LaaS) providers, such as BNPL platforms that plug into online shopping sites and others • Third-party debt capital providers to enable nondeposit takers to lend

Market structure
• Nimble competitors have taken market share from traditional banks and broadened access to borrowers previously underserved by banks. • Incumbent financial institutions can catch up, leveraging scale economies, existing customer bases, privileged trust positions, and (sometimes) access to financial infrastructures. • Entry of fintech start-ups as well as Big Tech firms make the market more contestable but potentially more concentrated as larger players leverage economies of scale in customer networks, data, and capital and tie financial services to other digital services.

Financial infrastructure
• Digital payments have become a key infrastructure element for digital lenders. • Open data frameworks are foundational infrastructure for alternative credit scoring. Fintech can tap into credit information systems including traditional bureaus and providers of alternative data. • Data privacy and consumer protection of data use become equally foundational as tech platforms seek to leverage user data and data from other sources to perform, market services, and engage in collections. • Necessary infrastructure includes both the legal and regulatory frameworks as well as technical implementations of registries for movable assets and invoices and off-balance-sheet financing vehicles. • Ancillary services such as trust management and backup servicing become increasingly important for smoothly functioning markets.

Source: Original elaboration for this publication.
Note: BNPL = buy-now-pay-later; B2B = business-to-business; NBFI = nonbank financial institution.

investors in equity, bond, and other markets, such as real estate and crypto-assets. That overall positive impact has also been accompanied by some instances of volume concentrations and market volatility as well as consumer protection lapses. In the business-to-business (B2B) fintech space, open banking applications are allowing account-to-account payment providers to replace debit networks and clearinghouse payments processing, and credit analytics innovators are providing banks and other lenders with options to replace both internal processes and traditional scoring services.

Now that fintech's cross-cutting impacts on the various dimensions of market outcomes have been discussed, this chapter turns to the impacts on each of the four market dimensions.

Financial Infrastructure

Financial infrastructure has advanced significantly alongside physical information and communication technology (ICT) infrastructure and mobile telephony.

Faster payment systems (FPS) are enabling new business models for payment services. They enable real-time payment to the payee and are accessible through a range of innovative payment channels, such as mobile apps and simplified processes (for example, using QR codes). This function enables licensed payment service providers to innovate the user experience, spurs competition between card-based payment services and bank account–based payment services, and enables integration with customers' social and economic lives.

Digital ID

Digital identification (ID) enables fintech firms and incumbent financial institutions alike to implement remote, convenient, and lower-cost customer interactions and data exchange without compromising safety. As noted in the Fintech Market Participants Survey conducted for this publication, incumbent and fintech firms alike expect a significant shift of sales, customer onboarding, and customer interactions from physical to online modes (Feyen et al. 2022b). Achieving this requires widespread development and adoption of digital ID services.

A well-designed digital ID enables remote identity validation, consent, and document signing. This allows the exchange of data held by other financial institutions (for example, bank statements); other businesses (for example, sales or purchase data); and potentially government agencies (for example, tax data and demographic information). Such exchanges can enable a financial institution to meet due diligence requirements not simply to onboard customers but also to assess creditworthiness and suitability for certain financial services like investment (for example, by validating net worth).

The increasing role of digital identity and data in financial services is motivating the development of a new class of financial infrastructures. Digital ID is becoming an integral part of the value chain of many fintech models; as such, market infrastructures for facilitating the provision and validation of digital IDs are emerging. These take the form of bringing together providers and consumers of digital ID services and enable customers to assert their identity digitally across different service providers in a seamless manner. Examples include FranceConnect, eHerkenning in the Netherlands, and the National Digital ID (NDID) platform in Thailand.

Similarly, as the scale and range of data being used increases, new market infrastructures are needed to orchestrate the consent-based exchange of data. These data exchange platforms are now emerging in many countries as the implementation of open banking and open finance frameworks expands. Examples include the Singapore Financial Data Exchange (SGFinDex) and India's Data Empowerment and Protection Architecture (DEPA).

Credit Information

Credit information systems are fundamental to sound lending, and they both benefit from and contribute to trends in data and fintech lending.[2] Data from credit registries and credit bureaus can ensure sound lending and help prevent overindebtedness. However, these traditional credit information providers may not have broad coverage of individuals and SMEs, particularly in EMDEs and among previously excluded segments. Fintech solutions using Big Data and advanced analytics have filled that gap, enabling lending to thin-file or no-file borrowers. The broad participation of lenders in a modern, open credit information infrastructure facilitates sound digital lending.

Secured-Assets Infrastructure

Digital invoicing, asset registries, and other infrastructure for secured transactions and asset-based lending are increasingly important drivers of fintech lending. Secured lending instruments can reduce credit risk and broaden access to finance beyond those who have traditional collateral (for example, real estate or fixed assets). The introduction of digital asset registries enables fintech lenders to secure loans via automated processes, increasing efficiency and reducing barriers to finance for many borrowers. Lending against digital invoices that have been registered on a central platform opens access to working-capital credit for small businesses that might not be creditworthy themselves but are owed a payment by a larger, more creditworthy company.

Platform-based models for the provision of financial services strongly resemble financial infrastructure. Platform-based models are emerging in areas like lending (for example, marketplace lending); investment (for example, mutual fund distribution platforms); insurance (for example, insurance distribution platforms); factoring (for example, national reverse factoring platforms in India and Mexico); and payments (for example, bill payment platforms and application programming interface [API] hubs). These, like a traditional financial infrastructure, serve the industry or market as a whole; they facilitate the offering of financial products but neither provide it nor compete with its participants, and they are expected to be seen as neutral with no preference for any particular participant or provider.

Accordingly, they also pose similar policy and regulatory issues to those of traditional financial infrastructure. As such, it is possible that these would formally get structured as financial infrastructure and might even be integrated into existing financial infrastructure.

New Business Models and Products

Reduced economic frictions, reconfigured financial value chains, new opportunities for entry, and shifting economies of scale and scope have resulted in the introduction of new products and business models. Fintech firms are proving nimble at leveraging data, connectivity, and improved processing capacity as well as at converting regulatory barriers into solvable technology challenges. Payments benefit strongly from the revolution in connectivity and have seen particularly rapid innovation, including in the area of international remittances. Incumbents have been slower to innovate, but many are catching up, leveraging their advantages in trust capital and regulatory position and often partnering with fintech companies to use, or provide, B2B services. Big Tech firms compound the advantages of fintech firms, leveraging their large-scale existing customer bases, customer data, and consumer trust. Technology platforms have increasingly embedded financial services into their core offerings.

Small businesses have been important beneficiaries of the digital transformation of finance. As small merchants participate more in e-commerce, they develop data trails and may benefit from the embedded finance provided by online marketplaces. Separately, digitally enabled efficiencies, tailoring, and risk mitigation have made SME finance a more viable market, with many fintech firms emerging to serve this segment.

A few insights from these market developments (discussed further in appendix A) bear highlighting.

Redefinition of "banking." The atomization of services, recombination of value chains, and financial services provision by small-focused players and Big Tech firms alike calls into question the essence of banking or what it could be. Is it deposit taking, or maintaining an account ledger, or enabling borrowing, or making a credit decision? In a world where each component of a financial service may be provided by a different entity, what matters most, and where should regulators focus—on the entity with the customer interface, the balance sheet, the data, the underwriting engine, the payment network, or the servers that are powering all of it? Should the financial sector be considered a distinct sector when finance is embedded in so many other activities? Regulators can mandate that certain activities be conducted only by specific providers; however, from the customer perspective, traditional financial providers may become less and less visible.

Limitations of data analytics. Data-driven business models can scale rapidly, but data analytics is not a panacea. The positive feedback loops from customer activity that generates data being used to provide additional services that generate more data, combined with network effects of many digital businesses, can enable rapid growth. These data can be used for targeted marketing, product tailoring, and credit screening. However, despite the thousands of unique data elements that many fintech lenders claim to analyze, most models rely on a small subset of those elements that tend to correspond to traditional credit underwriting approaches. Cash flows, consistency of location, and performance in repaying an initial small loan may be gathered from mobile money transactions and Global Positioning System (GPS) data but need to map to current account, address, and credit history.

Credit analyses are still better at comparing historical patterns than predicting the future, particularly after a structural break. In an extreme demonstration of this, the COVID-19 pandemic shifted the prospective profitability of whole industries and the incomes of countless businesses and individuals. Lenders who resumed lending without recalibrating their artificial intelligence (AI) models ran into trouble quickly.

Big Tech as both market disruptor and inclusion driver. Big Tech's ability to embed a tailored payment, loan, insurance, or other financial service into any economic, business, or social activity is both a powerful disruptor of traditional financial services and a potential driver of financial inclusion. Knowing the transaction context and the borrower's history, linking a loan to an underlying business activity, and being able to take repayment directly out of the cash flows and potentially to sanction a defaulting borrower—such as by limiting access to the marketplace, in the case of e-commerce lending—all allow the embedded finance provider to more closely control risk or to balance credit risk against other business objectives in ways that a bank cannot, without requiring prior credit history.

Competitive advantages of embedded finance. Embedded finance has intrinsic advantages over third-party lending that enable Big Tech firms to compete strongly in credit markets. Big Tech platforms have customers and their data, control transaction flows, and create enough value from core activities to cross-subsidize credit. In the case of buy-now-pay-later lending, for example, the seller often covers the cost of the short-term credit to the consumer to increase sales.

E-commerce platforms also make working capital available to merchants to increase the merchants' volume of business through the marketplaces. This working capital is not provided for free, but it does not have to earn the same net interest margin that a bank would require to generate a similar risk-adjusted return on capital, particularly since the bank's risk would be higher as it lacks the contextual data, collections, and sanctions capabilities.

In the aftermath of the COVID-19 pandemic, lenders closest to the underlying economic activity can more easily resume lending and contribute to resilience. The pandemic disrupted economies in ways that have obviated the value of prior credit history, which have slowed the resumption of conventional lending. Because supply chain finance and embedded finance have more direct visibility into borrowers' current activities and cash flows, they can help manage the risks at every stage—from ex ante credit screening and analysis through disbursement and collections—better than most third-party lenders (box 3.1). This linkage of banking and commerce could play an important role in economic resilience and recovery (World Bank 2022).

New Players: Entry, Concentration, and Competition

The sheer number of entrants and innovators is indicative of competitive pressures on traditional providers. By one compilation, there were more than 26,000 fintech start-ups globally in 2021 (as of November 2021), up from 12,100 in 2018.[3] Although fintech credit is not yet systemic, fintech lenders are significant in certain segments—for example, micro lending in Kenya and retail and small business in China and several developed markets. In the year before the pandemic, fintech firms' share of US consumer credit (38 percent) had exceeded the share of traditional banks (28 percent) (Rooney 2019). Competitive pressure from new entrants could change the behavior of incumbents, which may, for example, take on more risk as they seek to compensate for revenue losses. Supervisors should be attuned to this dynamic.

Competition and Concentration

Financial services are thus becoming more competitive but also potentially more concentrated. The entry of thousands of fintech start-ups as well as new licensing regimes for challenger banks, digital banks, alternative lenders, and others speak to that competitive pressure.

BOX 3.1
Fintech and the COVID-19 Pandemic

The pandemic accelerated the adoption of technologies across activities, from remote meetings to telehealth to e-commerce. Financial services providers, like other businesses, were forced to find ways to operate and service clients remotely. The increased use of digital platforms for commerce, logistics, and other activities is generating data, linkages, behaviors, and skills that can enable traditional lenders and new entrants to address some of the challenges of lending into the uncertainties of the pandemic's recovery phase, including lending to small and medium enterprises (SMEs).

Increases in Mobile Money, Other Digital Financial Services
The Global System for Mobile Communications Association (GSMA), a mobile network association, reports that the number of registered mobile money users increased by 13 percent globally in 2020, double the forecasted rate (GSMA 2021a). Growth was attributed in part to pandemic relief, which many governments delivered through mobile payments. For example, digital government-to-person (G2P) payments for garment sector workers in Bangladesh were enabled by opening 2.5 million accounts in less than a month, leveraging prior regulatory changes that allowed remote account opening.[a]

The World Bank's Business Pulse Surveys and Enterprise Surveys also documented an increase in the use of digital platforms during the pandemic.[b] Adoption of digital payments in emerging markets and developing economies (EMDEs) surged, as did downloads of digital banking apps (see appendix A). Digital connectivity to clients and alternative delivery channels changed almost overnight from a "nice to have" to a "must have," according to the Fintech Market Participants Survey conducted for this report. More than 80 percent of the survey respondents indicated that COVID-19 had increased the need for fintech and digital transformation (Feyen et al. 2022b). A survey of International Finance Corporation (IFC) clients on the early impacts of COVID-19 found a significant increase in prioritization of digitizing channels and internal processes and data analytics (IFC 2021).

In Nigeria, LAPO Microfinance Bank—a state microfinance bank originating from efforts of the Lift Above Poverty Organisation (LAPO)—leveraged its agent network to continue providing basic services to customers during an early lockdown period that shut down branch operations. After an initial decline in volumes, activity recovered and grew to more than double the precrisis levels by August 2020. In Colombia, Contactar, a microfinance institution serving rural areas, had seen low digital adoption before March 2020. Faced with lockdowns, Contactar expanded its use of local payment agents, internet payments, and WhatsApp client contact; together these efforts increased the adoption of alternative channels, maintained customer engagement, and improved loan repayment rates. In Peru, Caja Arequipa introduced the first fully digital loan for microentrepreneurs during the lockdown.

(Continued)

Fintech and the COVID-19 Pandemic *(continued)*

Boosts to Data and Product Innovation

The World Bank's *World Development Report 2022: Finance for an Equitable Recovery* points out that the pandemic rendered most traditional credit data irrelevant because credit histories did not reflect the pandemic's impact on a borrower's finances (World Bank 2022). Alternative data such as real-time transactions data from payments, inventory orders, and sales provide more visibility to current business performance and cash flows.

Technology-enabled innovations in product design can also help lenders manage the risks of lending into the recovery. Short-term, small-value loans; secured lending; supply chain finance; and embedded finance are forms of lending that enable financial services providers to tailor products and services to clients' needs while managing risk exposure through continuous, real-time monitoring of movable assets, invoices, inventory, orders, sales, payments, and other collateral and data.

Leveraging the data inherent in embedded finance can also improve visibility into borrowers' underlying economic activities. Embedded-finance lenders may be motivated to take on more risk than third-party lenders since the loan generates revenue streams for the lender via the core business transaction. An example is supply chain finance, through which anchor manufacturers were able to shore up their distribution networks during the pandemic, and large buyers ensured that their suppliers had access to finance. Data from the first half of 2020 showed that 10 leading global consumer goods manufacturers increased their outstanding debt by US$45 billion in the first half of 2020 to inject working capital into their supply chains, taking on the credit risk of their supply chain counterparties that banks or other lenders may not have been willing to assume (Dunbar and Singh 2020).

a. Bangladesh data from "Advancing Digital Inclusion for All," Bill and Melinda Gates Foundation's Goalkeepers website: https://www.gatesfoundation.org/goalkeepers/the -work/accelerators/financial-inclusion/.
b. Findings from the World Bank's COVID-19 Business Pulse Survey Dashboard (updated March 7, 2022), https://www.worldbank.org/en/data/interactive/2021/01/19/covid-19 -business-pulse-survey-dashboard; and Cirera et al. (2021).

Most Fintech Market Participants Survey respondents expect increased competition and lower barriers to entry (Feyen et al. 2022b). Most also expect markets to become more concentrated (figure 3.3). These views are consistent with a bifurcated market in which lower barriers to entry increase competition for smaller players or in specific segments, while economies of scale and network effects drive consolidation among large multiproduct institutions such as big banks and larger fintech and Big Tech firms. The forces that might lead to that configuration are discussed in the next section ("Implications for Market Structure").

FIGURE 3.3 Expected Shifts in Financial Market Concentration, by Subsector

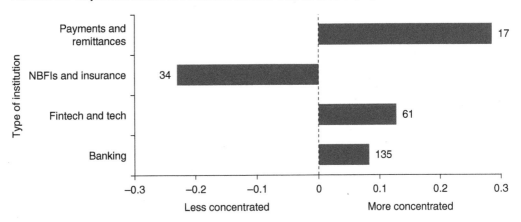

Source: Feyen et al. 2022b.

Note: Responses have been aggregated across product lines and responding institution type. Numbers next to the bars represent the number of respondents. The net concentration expectation for each responding institution type is a figure between −1 (least concentrated) and 1 (most concentrated), representing the average sentiment based on responses to this question: "How will the market structure of your key product markets evolve in the medium term (next 5 years) in terms of number of providers?" "Banking" includes large banks, small and medium banks, and multinational financial institutions. The Fintech Market Participants Survey, conducted May 2020 to January 2021, included 330 respondents from 109 countries across all six World Bank Group regions as well as high-income countries. The figure excludes 83 nonresponses from the various categories. For more information, see Feyen et al. (2022b) or the summary in appendix B. NBFI = nonbank financial institution.

Customer Relationships

Who "owns" the consumer relationship is in flux. Marketplaces, mobile banking, super-apps (apps providing an access channel to multiple services), product-specific apps, and digital banks are offering customers a variety of ways to engage with one or many financial services providers. Customers are balancing their options: they can choose multiple providers and assemble their own packages of services (aggregation via a smartphone screen with different apps), or they can opt for the convenience of a prepackaged set of services from either a traditional package (aggregation by the bank) or a new provider (aggregation via a marketplace or super-app).

Fintech Market Participants Survey respondents expressed strong expectations that new types of providers—digital banks, fintech firms, or marketplace aggregators—will dominate customer relationships (figure 3.4, panel a), and a plurality of respondents think customers will choose to have multiple relationships (figure 3.4, panel b). Although most bank respondents (54 percent) expect that customers will maintain a single core relationship, only a minority of banks (32 percent) expect that single relationship to be with a traditional bank (Feyen et al. 2022b).

Given the likelihood of shifting customer relationships, the survey respondents see digital transformation as posing substantial risks of customer loss and profit reduction in traditional market segments (Feyen et al. 2022b). Fintech and tech companies see this as less of a risk. Across all segments, however, the

FIGURE 3.4 Expectations about Customer Relationships in Financial Services, by Subsector

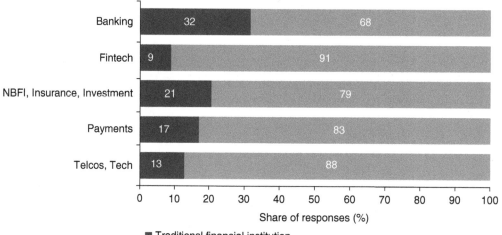

a. Relationship with traditional financial institutions versus new types of providers

Share of responses (%)

- ■ Traditional financial institution
- ■ New financial institution or marketplace aggregator or multiple providers

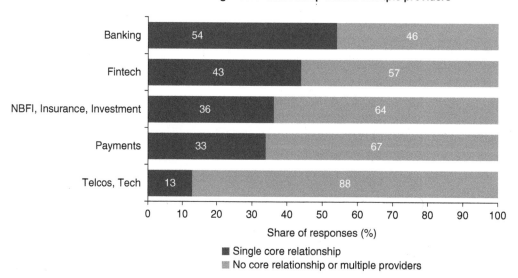

b. Single core relationship versus multiple providers

Share of responses (%)

- ■ Single core relationship
- ■ No core relationship or multiple providers

Source: Feyen et al. 2022b.
Note: The Fintech Market Participants Survey asked respondents their views on customer preferences over the medium term (the next five years) along two dimensions: (panel a) whether relationships would focus on traditional or new providers, and (panel b) whether customers will have a single core relationship or use multiple providers (directly or via a marketplace or platform player). "Banking" includes large banks, small and medium banks, and multinational financial institutions. "Aggregator" refers to a third-party institution that enables acquiring institutions to reach smaller merchants. The third party maintains the direct relationship with the smaller merchants and handles much of the operations and servicing aspects. The survey, conducted May 2020 to January 2021, included 330 fintech market participants from 109 countries across all six World Bank Group regions as well as high-income countries. For more information, see Feyen et al. (2022b) or the summary in appendix B. NBFI = nonbank financial institution; telcos = telecommunications companies.

FIGURE 3.5 Expected Risk of Customer Loss, Risk to Profits, and Potential for Cost Reduction from Fintech and Digital Transformation, by Subsector Type

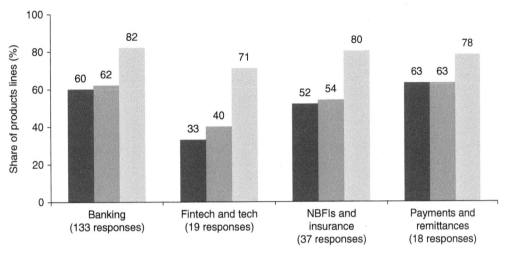

Source: Feyen et al. 2022b.

Note: The figure represents responses to this question in the Fintech Market Participants Survey: "To what extent are your business lines affected by digital transformation of the market?" The percentages represent aggregated averages across responding institution types and product lines. "Banking" includes large banks, small and medium banks, and multinational financial institutions. The survey, conducted May 2020 to January 2021, included 330 fintech market participants from 109 countries across all six World Bank Group regions as well as high-income countries. The figure excludes 123 nonresponses from the various subsector categories. For more information, see Feyen et al. (2022b) or the summary in appendix B. NBFIs = nonbank financial institutions.

respondents expect that digital transformation will reduce costs (figure 3.5). Taken together, this suggests that prices for consumers could fall, because if costs decline and profitability does not increase, the surplus in a competitive market would go to customers.

Implications for Market Structure

Market structure outcomes will depend on how three factors balance in a given market:

- *Degree of scale and scope economies* in a particular product or market

- *Customer preferences for choice* among many tailored products from different providers versus the convenience of preassembled product sets

- *Regulatory stances* on entry, licensing, and competition.

Scale and Scope Economies: Effects on Market Concentration and Inclusiveness

These processes could drive a range of industry structure outcomes. On the one hand, digital technology enables niche providers to reach a target customer base and be economically viable. On the other hand, customer acquisition, funding, "assembly," and switching costs tend to favor larger providers.

Without regulatory interventions to prevent entry, restrict crossover activities, or break up larger players, one likely outcome is a "barbell" configuration composed of relatively few large, multiproduct players on one end of the spectrum and many niche players on the other (figure 3.6). The large, multiproduct players could include traditional financial institutions as well as fintech and Big Tech firms—thus, both incumbents and new entrants. Small players may include fintech firms as well as geographically or sector-focused incumbents.

A barbell is not the only potential outcome but also is a central case given the economic forces at work; it gives rise to important policy issues regarding competition, regulatory perimeters, and ensuring a level playing field. Both the analytical barbell model and the industry views captured in the Fintech Market Participants Survey suggest that the concentration risks in financial services may increase despite the increasing entry of new players. The data-driven advantages of large players could increase switching costs and lock in customers; hence ex ante remedies by the sector regulators may be superior to ex post remedies. As a result, reinforcing competition will require taking both horizontal and vertical views of the financial services landscape as well as the cooperation of financial, sectoral, and competition authorities.

The interplay of technology, market forces, and policy will also influence the inclusiveness of market outcomes. Mobile connectivity is very high for low- and middle-income countries,[4] but an estimated 600 million individuals in these countries lack internet access, and broadband affordability is a barrier for many more (World Bank 2021). Digital business models can drive down costs so that even small markets offer sufficient scale for a provider to be viable; however, such providers may have difficulty competing with cross-border entrants that can offer services remotely and leverage larger markets to achieve scale and scope economies.

Limited access to cloud computing infrastructure may force policy makers to make trade-offs between financial services efficiency, resilience, and data

FIGURE 3.6 Potential "Barbell" Financial Services Market: An Illustration

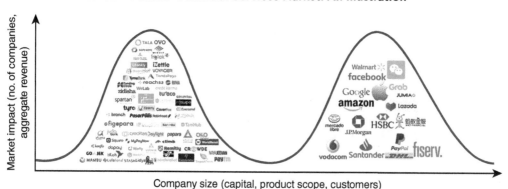

Company size (capital, product scope, customers)

Source: Feyen et al. 2022a.

Note: The figure is purely illustrative and does not constitute endorsement of particular companies' potential roles in financial services or projections as to their future size or success.

localization, particularly in smaller markets. The costs to authorities to effectively supervise a large number of small entities can also be significant and may be burdensome for EMDEs.

Emerging Risks and the Roles for Regulation

Promotion of fair competition. Concerns about market concentration must be addressed in a balanced way. Some issues, particularly regarding data abuse by Big Tech firms, are already crystallizing. Concentration in and of itself, however, is not necessarily a problem. The emergence of a monopoly may not indicate exclusionary practices but rather powerful network effects that create benefits to consumers from participating on the same platform (for example, on social media or messaging). A barbell configuration can manifest high concentration alongside product choice and price competition. Entry regulations that enable the development of a reservoir of potential competitors can keep markets contestable and forestall some types of market abuses by dominant players.

In some markets, concentration can lead to more intense beneficial competition, with a positive impact on price and quality. In many EMDEs, the banking sector is already concentrated; additional competition, even from a dominant technology player, would increase consumer choice. Product tying—that is, selling one product or service as a mandatory addition to purchase of another product or conditioned on earlier purchase of another product—as well as cross-subsidies can benefit consumers in terms of convenience and cost. In the EMDE context, concentrated mobile money markets have delivered strong welfare benefits. However, market concentrations give unregulated entities significant control over access to a marketplace or to large troves of personal data, and abuses have occurred in some markets. Furthermore, Big Tech crossovers into finance mean that monopoly power that might have been beneficial in one market can now be wielded, potentially detrimentally, in another. The balance struck between competition policy enforcement and efficiency and inclusion goals will vary across countries and across subsectors within countries at different stages of market development.

Oversight of entries, exits, and new business models. Regulators have struggled to supervise new business models, and the sheer numbers of new financial services entrants have inevitably led to firm failures and frauds (Gispert et al. 2022). Exit of some firms is part of a healthy innovation ecosystem and is not cause for concern if customer funds have been appropriately segregated and the wind-down is orderly—which has not always been the case.

Fraud is another matter. P2P lending in China grew very quickly from its start in 2007 to its peak in 2016, when over 4,000 platforms were active (Gispert et al. 2022). Numerous instances of fraud and Ponzi schemes (by some accounts, up to 40 percent of platforms were problematic) resulted in customer losses. Oversight was tightened, the industry shrank, and eventually P2P marketplaces were mandated to convert to regulated small loan providers. In Europe, two prominent failures—of Wirecard, a payments processor, and Greensill, a tech-enabled invoice financing operation—illustrate the challenges to regulators in adequately supervising complex fintech business models (Gispert et al. 2022). These fraudulent schemes have led to outright losses of capital as well as to losses of access to funds (for example, when accounts were frozen at other fintech firms that used Wirecard).

Consumer protection. Adequate regulation and supervision to protect consumers and foster trust in fintech must address not only soundness but also integrity, safety, and appropriateness. If properly designed and regulated, remote onboarding and automated KYC checks can help prevent illicit actors from gaining access to the financial system (Gispert et al. 2022). Yet the broader attack surface of a more diverse and fragmented financial system, and the extension of access points to untrained users, creates cybersecurity risks. Mundane examples are common—for example, of an illiterate mobile money user who gives a personal identification number (PIN) to the agent and later finds that an unexpected transfer was made. More sophisticated hacks—such as the automated transfer of bank funds to 1,500 fraudulently registered SIM cards in Uganda (URN 2020)—are also becoming increasingly common.

Fintech could pose significant consumer protection risks owing to the novelty and opaqueness of business models, unclear responsibilities of fintech entities, misaligned interests of fintech firms and consumers, lack of financial literacy, and challenges posed by digital finance for disclosures and transparency, as follows (Boeddu and Chien 2022):

- Consumers might misunderstand the product offering—for example, mistaking investing in crowdfunding platforms as providing guaranteed returns.

- The role of fintech entities regarding exceptional circumstances could be unclear—for example, lack of liquidity at e-money agent locations, fees and charges levied by agents, or who is responsible for customer service or tracking a misdirected payment.

- In some contexts, fintech or Big Tech entities might have a conflict of interest—for example, a platform might steer consumers to providers who pay higher commissions to the platform.[5]

- Inadequate safeguards for data protection and cybersecurity could expose consumers to unauthorized disclosure of their data, data breaches, and fraud perpetrated using stolen data.

- Extensive use of analytics and algorithms could perpetuate latent biases or inadvertent exclusion due to lack of data or technology access.

- Failures of fintech entities could expose consumers to loss of their funds, including those in transit, and complex partnership and outsourcing relationships may make it difficult for consumers to identify the responsible party and obtain resolution.

In situations where fintech is broadening inclusion by offering new products to customers with little experience of financial services, standards for responsible finance are critical. Although customers almost always receive a formal disclosure, and some kind of consent is required—for example, when the app is downloaded—few consumers read such disclosures and user agreements in full. Most cannot be said to have provided truly informed consent to the terms, as noted in the Regulation Note prepared for this report (Gispert et al. 2022).

Mobile and online lending is one area requiring careful supervision. The popularity of mobile money in Kenya, for example, has led to broader financial inclusion but also to the blacklisting of numerous borrowers for defaults on nano-loans under US$10, the terms and requirements of which they may not have fully understood.[6] One of the responses of the Kenyan regulator was to block mobile lenders from recording defaults with the credit bureau. This approach could be ineffective and hurt digital and conventional lenders alike seeking to understand the full indebtedness of a potential borrower without addressing the product appropriateness issue.

In Indonesia, regulators concerned about aggressive debt collection practices by Chinese fintech lenders (for instance, using borrowers' cell phone contacts data) issued rules to restrict online lenders from using all but a narrow subset of phone data (Potkin, Zhang, and Diela 2018). This move disrupted the innovative underwriting models that had been leveraging phone data.

Challenges extend to developed markets as well, as demonstrated in the United Kingdom by the 583 percent annual percentage rate and aggressive collection practices of Wonga (a payday loan firm). A carefully considered approach to strengthening consumer credit codes is needed to balance innovation and access with consumer protection.

Notes

1. This transition will take time, partly because of customer familiarity with USSD codes and the tariffs as well as sometimes limited availability of internet access. A 2021 survey across five low- to middle-income markets in Africa and Asia found that more than 90 percent of transactions still use USSD codes despite smartphone penetration rates of 25–40 percent (Pon 2021). Patented in 1994, USSD is an interactive, menu-based technology that is supported on most mobile devices. USSD messages can be up to 182 alphanumeric characters long. USSD is similar to short message service (SMS) in that it sends short text-based messages; however, instead of text messages going from user to user, USSD messages travel from the user to the mobile network or vice versa. USSD creates a real-time connection, which allows for a two-way exchange of data between users and the network. This makes the technology more responsive than SMS. Also, like SMS, USSD works on standard phones, feature phones, and smartphones without the need to install any app or program, or access to mobile data (GSMA 2018).

2. In some markets, fintech lenders have been excluded from reporting to, or querying, credit registries and bureaus. That may be shortsighted because the expansion of unreported lending will only reduce the value of registry and bureau data as a picture of the borrower's overall indebtedness.

3. "Number of fintech startups worldwide from 2018 to February 2021, by region," Statista Research Department Data (published September 7, 2022), https://www.statista.com/statistics/893954/number-fintech-startups-by-region/.

4. International Telecommunication Union (ITU) data show connectivity of 105 percent, reflecting the fact that in many markets subscribers have more than one subscriber identity module (SIM) card. See "Mobile Cellular Subscriptions (per 100 People), 1960–2020," World Bank Data (from the ITU's World Telecommunication/ICT Indicators Database), https://data.worldbank.org/indicator/IT.CEL.SETS.P2.

5. Routing consumer securities transactions through market makers that pay for order flow is an example. See, for example, Bair (2021).

6. The term "nano-loan" does not have a precise definition but generally indicates a loan for even smaller amounts and tenor than a microloan.

References

Bair, Sheila. 2021. "SEC Needs to Find a Way to Curb Payment for Order Flow." *Financial Times*, September 8.

Boeddu, Gian, and Jennifer Chien. 2022. "Financial Consumer Protection and Fintech: An Overview of New Manifestations of Consumer Risks and Emerging Regulatory Approaches." Consumer Protection technical note for *Fintech and the Future of Finance*, World Bank, Washington, DC.

Capgemini Research Institute. 2020. "World Payments Report 2020." Report, Capgemini, Paris.

Capgemini Research Institute. 2021. "World Payments Report 2021." Report, Capgemini, Paris.

Cirera, Xavier, Marcio Cruz, Arti Grover, Leonardo Iacovone, Denis Medvedev, Mariana Pereira-Lopez, and Santiago Reyes. 2021. "Firm Recovery during COVID-19: Six Stylized Facts." Policy Research Working Paper 9810, World Bank, Washington, DC.

Cornelli, Giulio, Sebastian Doerr, Lavinia Franco, and Jon Frost. 2021. "Funding for Fintechs: Patterns and Drivers." *BIS Quarterly Review* (September 2021): 31–43.

Cornelli, Giulio, Jon Frost, Leonardo Gambacorta, Raghavendra Rau, Robert Wardrop, and Tania Ziegler. 2020. "Fintech and Big Tech Credit: A New Database." Working Paper No. 887, Bank for International Settlements, Basel, Switzerland.

Dunbar, Nicholas, and Manpreet Singh. 2020. "Consumer Goods Giants Grow Inventory, Extend Receivables amid Covid-19 Shift." EuroFinance article, September 1.

Feyen, Erik, Jon Frost, Leonardo Gambacorta, Harish Natarajan, and Matthew Saal. 2022a. "Fintech and the Digital Transformation of Financial Services: Implications for Market Structure and Public Policy." Market Structure technical note for *Fintech and the Future of Finance*, World Bank, Washington, DC.

Feyen, Erik, Harish Natarajan, Guillermo Galicia Rabadan, Robert Paul Heffernan, Matthew Saal, and Arpita Sarkar. 2022b. "World Bank Group Global Market Survey: Digital Technology and the Future of Finance." Fintech Market Participants Survey for *Fintech and the Future of Finance*, World Bank, Washington, DC.

Gispert, Tatiana Alonso, Pierre-Laurent Chatain, Karl Driessen, Danilo Palermo, and Ariadne Plaitakis. 2022. "Regulation and Supervision of Fintech: Considerations for EMDE Policymakers." Regulation technical note for *Fintech and the Future of Finance*, World Bank, Washington, DC.

GSMA (Global System for Mobile Communications Association). 2018. "Mobile Technologies for the SDGs: How Start-Ups and Mobile Operators in Emerging Markets Are Leveraging USSD Technology to Address Socio-Economic Challenges." Brochure, GSMA, London.

GSMA (Global System for Mobile Communications Association). 2020. "State of the Industry Report on Mobile Money 2019." GSMA, London.

GSMA (Global System for Mobile Communications Association). 2021a. "Mobile Money Accounts Grow to 1.2 Billion in 2020." Press release, March 24.

GSMA (Global System for Mobile Communications Association). 2021b. "State of the Industry Report on Mobile Money 2021." GSMA, London.

IFC (International Finance Corporation). 2021. "The Early Impact of COVID-19 on Financial Institutions: Insights from a Survey of IFC Financial Institution Clients." Summary note of survey findings, IFC, Washington, DC.

Pon, Bryan. 2021. "'Back in the U.S.S.D.': Most Smartphone Users—Especially Women—Don't Use Apps for Financial Services." Guest article, NextBillion.net, April 7. https://nextbillion.net/ussd-smartphones-women-financial-services/.

Potkin, Fanny, Shu Zhang, and Tabita Diela. 2018. "A Call to the Boss: Indonesia Contends with Aggressive Chinese Online Lenders." Reuters, September 21.

Rooney, Kate. 2019. "Fintechs Help Boost US Personal Loan Surge to a Record $138 Billion." CNBC (updated February 24). https://www.cnbc.com/2019/02/21/personal-loans-surge-to-a-record-138-billion-in-us-as-fintechs-lead-new-lending-charge.html.

URN (Uganda Radio Network). 2020. "Mobile Money Hacking: Shs 10bn Stolen Using 1,500 SIM Cards." *The Observer* (Kampala, Uganda), October 27.

World Bank. 2021. *World Development Report 2021: Data for Better Lives.* Washington, DC: World Bank.

World Bank. 2022. *World Development Report 2022: Finance for an Equitable Recovery.* Washington, DC: World Bank.

CHAPTER 4

Core Policy Objectives and Evolving Trade-Offs

Main Policy Challenges

Authorities are eager to foster the benefits of digital transformation, but they are also mindful of various challenges that emerge as digital transformation continues to permeate market activities. Fintech can promote poverty alleviation and economic growth by enhancing financial efficiency, inclusion, competition, and innovation; however, these benefits must be carefully weighed against challenges and risks such as those described in chapter 3. To that end, the Bali Fintech Agenda outlined by the World Bank Group and International Monetary Fund (IMF) advocates embracing the promise of fintech while managing risks to consumers and to the stability and integrity of the financial system (box 4.1).

Fundamentally, fintech-related risks are similar in nature to those of traditional financial activities, but their shape and materiality can differ significantly. Mitigating risks to core policy objectives—such as financial stability, integrity, and safety—is a precondition for reaping the benefits of fintech adoption. All forms of financial services provision ultimately may give rise to, among other things, liquidity, credit, market, and operational risks at the microprudential level and risks from system-level externalities at the macroprudential level.

Digital transformation causes these risks to present themselves in different ways and could also trigger risk migration outside of the regulatory perimeter. As such, several interrelated and heightened challenges stand out in several areas—challenges that will continue to evolve as the industry develops.

The Bali Fintech Agenda

The Bali Fintech Agenda—endorsed in 2018 by the Executive Boards of the World Bank Group and the International Monetary Fund—distills high-level issues for policy makers and the international community into 12 elements to help policy makers harness the benefits and opportunities of rapid advances in financial technology while also managing the risks (IMF and World Bank 2018). These elements broadly promote four objectives:

- *Foster an enabling environment to harness opportunities.* Develop open and accessible foundational infrastructures; reinforce fair competition and contestable markets to ensure a level playing field; and address challenges related to reach, customer information, and commercial viability to promote financial inclusion.
- *Strengthen the financial sector policy framework.* Monitor developments to formulate conducive policies and identify risks; adapt the regulatory framework and supervisory practices to promote the safe entry of new products and entities, maintain stability, and respond to risks; and provide greater legal clarity and certainty while removing unnecessary legal obstacles.
- *Address potential risks and improve resilience.* Safeguard consumer and investor protection; ensure financial and monetary stability as well as financial integrity; and develop resilient digital infrastructures to protect data integrity and privacy.
- *Promote international collaboration.* Encourage sharing of information and experiences and strengthen coordination for effective policy making.

Financial stability. Fintech developments can help diversify the financial sector and strengthen risk management, which may increase financial resilience and integrity. However, untested and potentially risky business models and new entrants, new financial interlinkages and interdependencies across the sector, and new concentration risks may pose challenges to financial stability.

Financial integrity. Fintech and digital identification approaches can improve transparency and reduce financial integrity risks. However, money laundering and financing of terrorism threats may increase when technology enables anonymity and instant global reach.

Consumer protection and data protection. A proliferation of new players and new business models can, in principle, enhance the consumer experience and make products safer because fintech enables tailoring to specific consumer needs and can better protect consumers and their data (for example, through encryption). However, so far this proliferation often has occurred in unregulated product areas, creating challenges to ensuring whether products are appropriate for different consumers as well as to ensuring that fraudsters are not among the new entrants.

Limited electronic disclosure of terms and conditions as well as lack of transparency on costs and business models create additional risks to consumers, particularly those who are less financially literate. Unauthorized disclosure and use of personal data, including identify theft, is another key challenge.

Pass-through compliance. In a partnership between fintech or Big Tech firms with incumbent financial institutions, the latter would be expected to ensure compliance with existing regulations but might not have the full visibility or ability to enforce it. When these incumbent institutions are smaller, they might be perceived to be lower risk under a risk-based supervision framework, and hence risk buildups could go unnoticed.

Operational and cybersecurity risks. The distribution of technology and access points to end users and the restructuring of value chains leads to increased complexity, more points of vulnerability, and broader attack surfaces for cybercriminals. Cyberattacks or failures necessitate strong operational resilience frameworks because they compromise business continuity, carry economic and reputational risks, and potentially threaten financial stability. Another source of elevated operational risk is the higher reliance on third-party service providers, such as for cloud storage and computing, data provision, and critical business services such as third-party payment processing services.

Competition. As described in chapter 3, owing to economies of scale, network effects, reputation, and capital, large providers such as Big Tech companies could achieve dominant positions quickly, thereby raising entry barriers and reducing overall competition or contestability. Market dominance by a limited number of providers could reduce consumer welfare. However, in markets where competition is limited, the entry of large providers could have important welfare gains and enhance competition in the short to medium term. How the market develops from that point will depend on the confluence of policy actions and market developments.

Regulatory arbitrage. Financial services have been offered by new entrants that largely operate outside of the regulatory perimeter, although their activities and risks are similar in nature to those offered by regulated entities. Similarly, decentralized systems, such as crypto-assets and peer-to-peer or decentralized finance (DeFi) platforms, may prove more difficult to regulate and supervise if a central governing body is absent. Given the supranational nature of some fintech solutions, cross-border arbitrage opportunities complicate matters further and call for more international coordination.

Policy for an Evolving Fintech Market

How policy goals regarding sound inclusive financial systems and competitive markets can be achieved depends on the entities providing financial services, the business models they use, and the market structure that ensues. The analysis here focuses on likely market structure outcomes based on underlying technology and economic drivers. It raises new issues for financial supervision, competition regulation, and consumer protection as (a) financial services move from the first phase of *disaggregation* and competition to a new phase of *reaggregation* and concentration alongside competitive entry and atomization, and (b) embedded finance has begun to demonstrate its power, particularly during the COVID-19 pandemic.

Regulating the Concentrated Market

Salient issues include how to regulate and supervise a growing number of new entrants and how to manage increasing concentration at the other end of the spectrum. On the consumer side, growing competition, entry of new players from unregulated sectors, and broadened inclusion of new customer segments all combine to create a dynamic where consumers' best interests may be lost in the rush for efficiency, market share, and revenues. The raft of new, smaller entrants challenges financial supervisors to review the regulatory perimeter and to become more adept at monitoring and supervising—and leveraging digital tools in regulatory technology (regtech) and supervisory technology (suptech), where appropriate.

The reaggregation and emerging concentration of market power introduces challenges in managing both the systemic risks and the market-conduct risks of an emerging set of large and potentially important global players whose activities cut across banking and nonfinancial businesses. For example, concentrated infrastructure providers serving the financial sector, such as cloud services and digital payments networks, present potential systemic concentrations of operational risk. A hardware failure at one payments network left millions unable to pay with their cards for about five hours across Europe in June 2018 (Bank of England 2019; Togoh and Topping 2018). The Financial Stability Board and other standard-setting bodies are doing further work in this area to provide guidance on addressing concentration risks (see, for example, Crisanto et al. 2019; FSB 2019).

Regulating the Embedded-Finance Market

The proliferation of cross-sector players highlights the challenge of interpreting monopoly guidelines in a new era. Concentration may not imply monopoly power in a highly contestable market, and the relevant market is increasingly difficult to define where traditional financial services providers compete with fintech and Big Tech companies in specific product areas.

Product tying—part of many platform and embedded-finance value propositions—illustrates the growing complexity of balancing consumer protection with financial and competition regulation as business models and market structures evolve. Although cross-selling services has long been a common strategy in the financial sector, it has been subject to explicit anti-tying provisions in many markets. For example, a credit line was not supposed to be linked to requiring the borrower to move its transaction account to the lender.

Unbundling of financial services would tend to reduce anticompetitive product tying. Reaggregation and embedded finance, in contrast, put tying at the center of financial product economics. In multisided technology platforms, linking, cross-selling, and cross-subsidizing of products has generated both consumer benefits (for example, "free" email accounts tied to advertising) and potentially questionable practices (for example, search engines charging businesses for advertising and favorable search ranking). Now cross-selling is extending across financial and nonfinancial services, potentially allowing for a firm's dominance in the nonfinancial services to extend to the financial sector as well.

These developments will test the boundaries of competition analysis and redefine how regulators consider the benefits and costs of concentration, product tying, and other aspects of market structure and conduct. Platform models that combine free services that have network effects with financial services could become highly concentrated and potentially result in abusive exercise of monopoly power, as examined in the Market Structure Note prepared for this report (Feyen et al. 2022). For example, a dominant social network that has a quasi-monopoly position over small local businesses' connections to their customers might embed payments in the social networking experience and make it difficult for a customer to pay businesses through anything other than the network's payment product.

For borrowers, the increased resilience and access potentially offered by embedded credit is largely the result of tying credit to other transactions. A distributor offering supply chain finance inevitably ties that working capital to the purchase of its products. What may seem to be low-cost or free tied services from a platform provider are rarely truly free; in many emerging markets and developing economies (EMDEs) however, incurring costs in terms of data sharing, loss of privacy, or product lock-ins may be acceptable to gain access to finance that is not otherwise available.

In some product areas, open data frameworks that eliminate data monopolies (for example, by conferring data ownership to the data subjects, who can then make their own data available to different finance providers) could help ensure that the benefits of innovative business models can be realized consistent with competitive markets and consumer protection. These data frameworks require a level of consumer financial and data literacy. As an alternative, data intermediaries might enable safe data sharing; they could also help individuals better understand and enforce their rights over their personal data (World Bank 2021).

Balancing the Policy Trade-Offs

More broadly, policy makers will have to address increasingly complex trade-offs that depend on the level of development of the financial system and its customers, the preexisting competitive environment, and other social preferences. The Market Structure technical note prepared for this publication describes the complex policy trade-offs that may evolve in conjunction with the rapid developments in the financial sector (Feyen et al. 2022). Fast-paced technological innovation and its impact on the industry suggest that balancing trade-offs may become more challenging, especially for EMDEs with capacity constraints and multiple competing mandates, including the following:

- Financial stability and market integrity

- Efficiency and competition

- Data privacy and consumer protection.

For example, financial inclusion, innovation, and efficiency objectives may run counter to preserving financial stability. Fintech companies may promote new lending based on weak business models, or they may be exposed to increased cyber risks. Big Tech platforms may offer significant efficiency and inclusion gains, but they can also quickly dominate markets and become too big to fail. Similarly, reaping the full innovation and efficiency gains of fintech may require gathering, processing, and exchanging large amounts of consumer data, which may run afoul of consumer and data safeguards and could increase financial integrity risks.

Different societies will attach different preferences to different market structure outcomes. Some societies may accept market structures that concentrate data and supercharge network effects if they reduce intermediation costs and broaden inclusion. In other markets, the resulting market power might be seen as more detrimental than these benefits. Concentration of infrastructure and data in state hands may be accepted in some societies, while others may be more concerned about the potential extension of state surveillance. As in other industries, regulators will have to balance the efficiencies of natural monopolies against potential abuse of market power.

These trade-offs also evolve as a country moves up the fintech development ladder. At lower levels of fintech development, the range of services, scale, and penetration is still limited. This limitation requires the willingness of policy makers to support innovation and provide basic legal and regulatory clarity. In these less-developed countries, addressing data gaps that prevent effective risk monitoring and taking measures to ensure that financial integrity objectives are met are key priorities because the risks to financial stability, fair competition, and consumer and investor protection are still relatively low.

However, as the scale, complexity, interconnectedness, and possible concentration of financial services increase in a given country, policy makers must focus more on safeguarding financial stability, data protection, and fair competition. This requires that legal, regulatory, and supervisory frameworks—as well as technology and financial infrastructures—be reviewed and strengthened accordingly to support a smooth transition to a flourishing fintech ecosystem that remains consistent with policy objectives. Figure 4.1 illustrates the policy trade-offs that result from fintech developments.

FIGURE 4.1 Policy Trade-Offs due to Fintech Developments

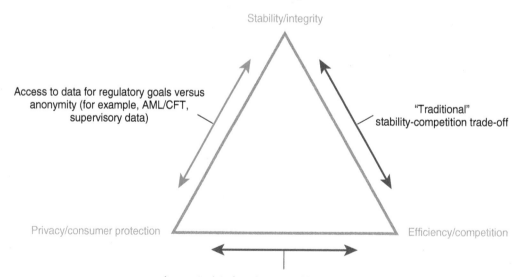

Source: Feyen et al. 2022.
Note: The figure illustrates the potential policy trade-offs between several competing mandates or objectives: (a) financial stability and market integrity, (b) efficiency and competition, and (c) data privacy and consumer protection. AML/CFT = anti–money laundering and combating the financing of terrorism.

References

Bank of England. 2019. "Bank of England Announces Supervisory Action over Visa Europe's June 2018 Partial Outage Incident." Press release, March 8.

Crisanto, Juan Carlos, Conor Donaldson, Denise Garcia Ocampo, and Jermy Prenio. 2019. "Regulating and Supervising the Clouds: Emerging Prudential Approaches for Insurance Companies." Insights on Policy Implementation No. 13, Financial Stability Institute, Basel, Switzerland.

Feyen, Erik, Jon Frost, Leonardo Gambacorta, Harish Natarajan, and Matthew Saal. 2022. "Fintech and the Digital Transformation of Financial Services: Implications for Market Structure and Public Policy." Market Structure technical note for *Fintech and the Future of Finance*, World Bank, Washington, DC.

FSB (Financial Stability Board). 2019. "Third-Party Dependencies in Cloud Services: Considerations on Financial Stability Implications." Report, FSB, Basel, Switzerland.

IMF (International Monetary Fund) and World Bank. 2018. "The Bali Fintech Agenda." Chapeau paper, September 19, IMF and World Bank, Washington, DC.

Togoh, Isabel, and Alexandra Topping. 2018. "Visa Outage: Payment Chaos after Card Network Crashes—As It Happened." *The Guardian*, June 1.

World Bank. 2021. *World Development Report 2021: Data for Better Lives*. Washington, DC: World Bank.

CHAPTER 5

Regulation and Supervision

Current Regulatory Environment

A high-quality policy environment is a necessary, but insufficient, condition for fintech development, as documented in the Fintech Activity Note prepared for this publication (Didier et al. 2022). The degree of fintech activity is consistently on the low end of the distribution in countries that score poorly on policy indexes capturing the existence of legal and regulatory frameworks relevant for digital financial services, whereas it varies widely across countries that score high on these indexes. Regarding the role of sector-specific legislation and regulations, the results are mixed: although the existence of laws and regulations for e-money, digital identification (ID), and e-signatures in support of electronic Know Your Customer frameworks tends to be positively associated with fintech activity, the coefficient on consumer protection tends to be negative.

The regulatory stance in different jurisdictions has sometimes facilitated or sometimes blocked these trends of technology-driven atomization, reconfiguration, and creation of open digital infrastructures. A notable example of facilitation was the Central Bank of Kenya's acquiescence to the creation of M-Pesa. In other markets, mobile money was restricted to bank providers and was slow to be implemented. The disaggregation of services and implementation of partnerships and outsourcing arrangements fundamental to this value chain restructuring depends on supervisory acceptance. Some regulators, for example, have provided detailed guidelines for banks' outsourcing arrangements.

The entry of new businesses and the introduction of new, technology-enabled business models depend on the approach regulators take. The Regulation technical note prepared for this publication highlights three prominent approaches: regulate, wait and see, or test and learn (Gispert et al. 2022). In the aftermath of the 2008–09 Global Financial Crisis, when banks were seen as having failed society, some regulators became more welcoming of innovative financial services, from digital banks or neobanks (which function only through an online presence) to new payment services and alternative lenders. For some innovations, simply standing to the side is sufficient; marketplace lending emerged in the interstices between banking and capital markets regulation. Other innovations require enabling laws or regulations. Connectivity and computing enable marketplaces for invoice financing and for lending against physical assets like solar panels, but these are viable business models only when supported by the appropriate legal and regulatory frameworks for secured transactions and asset-based lending.

The Fintech Market Participants Survey shows that a significant proportion of respondents in emerging markets and developing economies (EMDEs) feel there is scope to improve the regulatory and supervisory framework, although there is significant variation across regions and between incumbents and new entrants (Feyen et al. 2022). Among incumbents in high-income economies, perceptions are almost evenly split between viewing the regulatory framework as too tight or as about right (figure 5.1, panel a). In EMDEs, except in the Latin America and the Caribbean region, a significantly higher proportion of incumbents feel the regulatory framework is about right. Among new entrants, a similar trend is seen, although a considerable proportion of advanced economies feel the regulatory framework is too tight (figure 5.1, panel b).[1]

The Fintech Market Participants Survey shows that regulatory changes permitting electronic Know Your Customer and remote onboarding are seen as critical by both incumbents and new entrants (Feyen et al. 2022). In addition, the incumbents see policies enabling engagement of third-party agents as critical. Implementation of digital identification (ID) must be supported by appropriate regulatory changes. The survey also finds that a considerable proportion of incumbents and fintech companies alike feel that the regulatory frameworks for remote onboarding and account creation are inadequate in their jurisdictions.

Typology of Regulatory Responses

The regulatory approaches observed across jurisdictions (figure 5.2) can be broadly grouped as follows:

- *Applying existing regulatory frameworks* to new business models by focusing on the underlying economic function—for example, regulating digital currency exchanges as money services business or exchanges. Countries with legal and regulatory frameworks that are principles- and outcomes-based have found it easier to extend the applicability of existing frameworks.

- *Adjusting existing regulatory frameworks* to accommodate reengineering of existing processes and allow adoption of new technologies—for example, minor tweaks to allow market entry of digital-only banks (digital banks or neobanks), use of digital forms of ID to open accounts, and adoption of cloud computing for banking services along the lines of existing rules for outsourcing.

FIGURE 5.1 Views of Financial Market Participants on Whether the Regulatory Environment Enables Innovation by Incumbents and New Entrants, by Region

a. Regulators enable innovation by incumbents (% that agree)

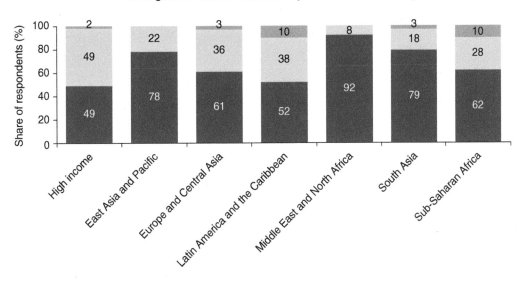

b. Regulators enable innovation by new entrants (% that agree)

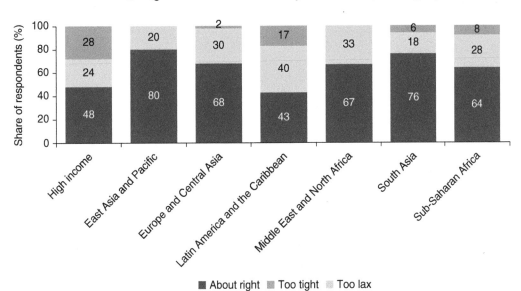

■ About right ▨ Too tight ▨ Too lax

Source: Fintech Market Participants Survey (Feyen et al. 2022).
Note: The figure represents responses to this question in the Fintech Market Participants Survey: "How would you characterize the overall regulatory and supervisory environment across your key markets with respect to enabling fintech and digital innovation by incumbents and new entrants?" The survey, conducted May 2020 to January 2021, included 330 fintech market participants from 109 countries across all six World Bank Group regions as well as high-income countries. For more information, see the Fintech Market Participants Survey note prepared for this publication (Feyen et al. 2022) or the summary of that note in appendix B.

FIGURE 5.2 Areas in Which Regulators Have Modified Regulatory and Supervisory Approaches to Facilitate Fintech Development or Develop Supervisory Capacity, by Country Income Level

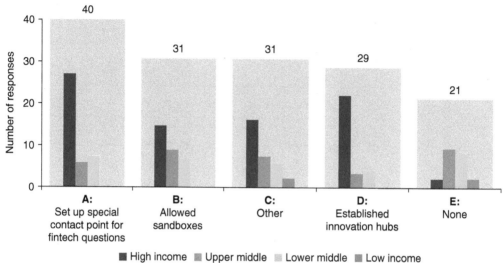

Source: IMF and World Bank 2019.
Note: The figure represents responses to the 2019 Global Fintech Survey from 96 jurisdictions. Respondents were asked, "Have authorities modified their regulatory and supervisory approach to facilitate the development of fintech and/or develop supervisory capacity?" Respondents checked all answers (A–E) that apply, hence the respective numbers of responses add up to more than 96. Numbers above the areas shaded in light gray the total number of jurisdictions that picked each respective response (A–E), and the bars indicate the share of responses by income group (defined according to World Bank classifications). The response rate varied both regionally and by the income level, with fewer responses from less-developed economies and the highest response rate from European authorities.

- *Creating new regulations* to extend regulatory perimeters and introduce specific requirements for new classes of players in the ecosystem—for example, creating a new class of regulated entities for e-money and marketplace lending platforms, and requiring bank providers to offer application programming interfaces (APIs) to allow other institutions to directly access information and provide services to customers (open banking).

- *Adopting new frameworks* to promote innovation and experimentation in areas where the regulatory framework is either unclear or not present. These frameworks include developments like the following:

  - *Regulatory sandboxes* are structured to allow for experimentation, albeit with restrictions imposed on the scale, duration, and scope to mitigate risk while allowing for demonstration of new technologies and approaches. The learning from regulatory sandboxes could then be used to structure the regulatory framework.

  - *Innovation hubs* seek to allow innovators to directly interface with regulators and industry experts to help mainstream innovations.

  - *Accelerators* seek direct financing to help demonstrate and bring to market new innovations.

Among the "new framework" approaches, regulatory sandboxes have captured the attention of several jurisdictions, spanning high-income economies (for example, Australia; China; Hong Kong SAR, China; Japan; the UK; and the US) and World Bank client countries (for example, China, Colombia, India, Indonesia, Jordan, Mexico, and Morocco). Some EMDEs have adopted innovation facilitators—notably, regulatory sandboxes to provide a pathway for fintech approaches that are within the spirit of the regulatory framework but not fully compliant with the letter of the regulation.

It is too early to determine the outcomes of the regulatory sandboxes in EMDEs. However, based on a review of the sandbox initiatives in a few jurisdictions, it appears that sandboxes are being used by both incumbents and new entrants. Incumbents are focused on adopting new processes like remote onboarding.

Activity-Specific Regulation

EMDEs have sought to bring specific fintech activities within the regulatory perimeter by developing customized regulations, either drawing on the general powers accorded to regulators or through provisions in public laws (figure 5.3).

FIGURE 5.3 **Areas in Which Regulators Have Modified Regulatory Frameworks to Address Emerging Risks from Fintech Activities, by Activity Type and Country Income Level**

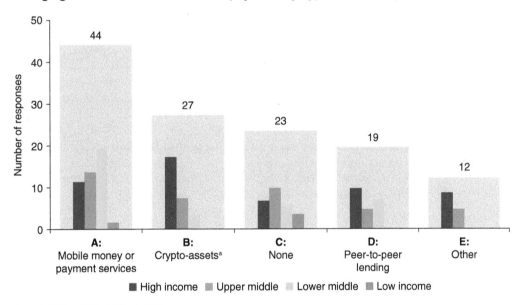

Source: IMF and World Bank 2019.
Note: The figure represents responses to the 2019 Global Fintech Survey from 96 jurisdictions. Respondents were asked, "In which areas have authorities modified their regulatory framework (e.g., expanding the perimeter or introducing a new regulation) to address emerging risks from fintech activities?" Respondents checked all answers (A-E) that apply, hence the respective numbers of responses add up to more than 96. Numbers above the areas shaded in light gray indicate the total number of jurisdictions that picked each respective response (A-E), and the bars indicate the share of responses by income group (defined according to World Bank classifications). The response rate varied both regionally and by the income level, with fewer responses from less-developed economies and the highest response rate from European authorities.
a. Regulated crypto-asset activities may include issuance, exchange, and custody.

Digital payments and e-money services. E-money issuance by nonbank entities, notably telecommunications operators, has been the dominant fintech activity in many EMDEs, several of which have accordingly modified their regulatory frameworks to enable e-money development.[2] In general, the approach has been to develop customized regulations covering both prudential and conduct aspects.

There has also been substantial convergence, particularly among EMDEs, on requiring companies outside of the financial sector that are offering e-money services to set up dedicated entities solely focused on e-money and associated payment services. The e-money entities are, however, allowed to originate sales of financial products for other regulated financial service providers.

Other fintech activities being brought within the regulatory perimeter include lending platforms. In some cases, this approach has followed a period of "wait and see" when these services were not regulated or followed an iterative process of providing basic regulatory frameworks and fine-tuning them—following the "test and learn" approach (further discussed in Gispert et al. 2022).

Digital banks. These services involving deposit taking are often permitted by a (sometimes temporary) extension of the banking licensing framework. Some jurisdictions have opted for a phased licensing process through which new entrants start operations with limited activities and finally become fully licensed banks. Regulators mainly focus on facilitating the authorization process. Some jurisdictions are starting to issue specific licensing frameworks for digital-only banks with restrictions on physical presence and requiring a focus on financial inclusion.

Crowdfunding platforms (marketplace finance). Lending platforms help connect investors with borrowers or corporates seeking to get funds by selling their equity or debt. Some countries have enacted a single framework to encompass both securities-based crowdfunding and lending crowdfunding. Other jurisdictions have opted for separate regimes, a model that seems more prevalent in countries with sector-based supervisory models.

Crypto-assets. Most countries have taken a cautious stance toward crypto-assets. Some have taken a balanced approach by proactively regulating crypto-asset activity without outright banning; some have banned some or all crypto-assets activities; and others have taken a wait-and-see approach.

In light of their cross-border and global nature, crypto-assets including stablecoins (crypto-assets whose value is pegged to the price of another asset such as the US dollar) pose international regulatory arbitrage risks. Standard-setting bodies are applying general and transparent principles in their guidance and standards. The treatment of crypto-asset activity should focus on economic functions and objectives, using a proportionate "same risk, same activity, same treatment" approach. At the same time, the approach should aim for simplicity and to ensure a future-proof, technology-neutral stance, which helps in turn to ensure a level playing field.

Data-Generation Issues: Possibilities and Perils

Technological innovation has spurred the increase of granular, real-time data, posing significant opportunities and challenges that call for a policy response (box 5.1). According to *World Development Report 2021: Data for Better Lives*

(World Bank 2021b), these innovations in data generation create new opportunities for enhancing the economic performance of firms; for repurposing data to improve the design, execution, and evaluation of public policies; and for helping individuals and communities make better choices by accessing more information and knowledge.

Balancing data protection with open banking. Because new ways of collecting, organizing, analyzing, and exchanging data are central to fintech, regulators must address the risks while ensuring fair access. Big Tech firms have largely relied on large troves of user data generated on their own platforms or acquired from third parties. Fintech firms, in contrast, have primarily gathered user data through their apps. Both Big Tech and fintech companies, however, had to gather data from customers of other financial institutions. As a result, fundamental data protection and privacy issues have prompted regulatory actions.

Many high-income economies and a few EMDEs have responded by formulating an overarching legal framework for general data protection and privacy and issuing open banking regulations. The overarching data protection and privacy frameworks cover issues related to the collection, access, and portability of personal information as well as principles related to data quality and rectification, lawful processing, purpose specification, and consent (IMF and World Bank 2019). Open banking regulations seek to require banks and, in some countries, other financial institutions as well (for example, in India and Mexico) to provide a minimum set of data in an online and automated manner to third parties authorized by the account holder (World Bank 2022). These third parties are brought within the financial sector regulatory perimeter.

Although most of the jurisdictions that have developed an open banking scheme already had a data protection framework in place, some have amended such frameworks (as in Australia), and others developed them after having already implemented an open banking scheme (World Bank 2022). Except in the United States, all high-income economies had a data protection framework before issuing open banking regulations. In countries where data protection frameworks do not exist (for example, the United States), the open banking scheme recognizes the need for a data-permissioned environment.

In India, following judicial rulings, a data protection framework was adopted in 2019. This framework includes the construct of "consent manager" and "data fiduciary" and provides a pathway for development of open banking (World Bank 2022). Nigeria and Rwanda issued payment regulations to allow for payment initiation service providers to access bank data in 2019. Appendix D summarizes the open banking framework adopted in these and other selected countries.

Balancing artificial intelligence with consumer protection. As for data processing, the application of artificial intelligence (AI) techniques has been shown to pose consumer protection risks and has prompted regulators and the industry alike to develop guidelines on the responsible use of AI. In addition, the reliance of AI on past or unrepresentative data could perpetuate embedded biases that may result in discrimination and exclusion (see, for example, Vigdor 2019). This has prompted calls for human oversight and better scrutiny of models and algorithms to better understand their inner workings and predictions. Regulators have thus far not intervened directly, although some have called for the adoption of a codes of conduct, and others have developed guidelines.[3]

World Development Report 2021: Data for Better Lives

Data can lead to better lives through multiple channels: governments can use data to improve programs, policies, and the targeting of scarce resources to marginalized people and areas. The private sector can use data to fuel platform-based business models that stimulate economic activity and international trade in services. Individuals, empowered by data, can make better decisions and hold governments accountable.

Data can also be subject to abuse through multiple channels: governments could use data to undertake political surveillance or target certain social groups for discrimination. Private sector actors could exploit market power arising from data to take advantage of their customers. Individuals could access data illegally for criminal purposes.

Governance arrangements to address such concerns remain in their infancy, particularly in lower-income countries. Legal and regulatory frameworks for data are incomplete, with gaps in critical safeguards (such as cybersecurity, data protection, and cross-border data flows) and a shortage of measures to enable data sharing (such as open licensing and interoperability). Even where nascent data governance frameworks exist, a dearth of institutions with the requisite administrative capacity, decision-making autonomy, and financial resources constrains their effective implementation and enforcement.

Source: World Bank 2021b.

Regulation for Fair Competition

Mobile money competition. In several EMDEs, competition issues notably concern access to telecommunications services, exclusive distribution arrangements, and unequal access to platforms. Mobile money issuance in EMDEs is largely led by telecommunications operators and is dependent on native telecommunications services like Unstructured Supplementary Service Data (USSD), a traditional transaction interface used on basic phones. EMDE banks also leverage these channels to offer mobile banking and mobile payment services. Nonbank mobile money issuers rely on the same channels. This situation has enabled telecommunications operators—who are also mobile money issuers, either their own or through a subsidiary or partnership with another financial institution—to exert control over channels to which other (non-telecommunications) providers need access to offer their services. This has given telecommunications operators pricing power and the ability to constrain competitors, which in turn has required interventions by telecommunications regulators or dedicated competition-related public authorities. For example, the Competition Authority of Kenya intervened to require telecommunications operators to establish fair and transparent access to USSD services (World Bank 2021a).

Competition issues have also arisen regarding the exclusivity of third-party distribution networks, like agents used by mobile money providers. In China, where Big Tech activity has been significant, preferential treatment of offerings by companies related to the platform provider has raised competition issues. For example, some have questioned the services of group companies in platform models—for example, the lack of diversity of money market funds made available to customers of the Alipay third-party mobile and online payment platform (World Bank 2022).

Big Tech advantages. Regulators have sought to adjust the regulatory framework to create space for Big Tech companies to provide financial services: e-money issuance, digital bank licenses, and open banking. E-money licenses have been leveraged by telecommunications operators in EMDEs, notably in Sub-Saharan Africa but also in other regions. Other Big Tech companies like Google, Facebook, Alipay, Tencent, and Grab and Gojek have obtained e-money licenses in various jurisdictions. Some jurisdictions, notably in Asia (such as China, the Republic of Korea, and Singapore), have also allowed Big Tech companies to be shareholders in digital banks. The other approach has been to leverage open banking regulations to allow Big Tech companies to manage the customer interface for initiating payments, such as through India's Unified Payments Interface (UPI).

These approaches, while subjecting Big Tech firms to conduct regulations, do not fundamentally address competition issues, which has prompted regulators to impose additional requirements. In India, Big Tech firms were able to leverage the third-party payment initiation capability to rapidly expand their presence in the payments market, prompting the imposition of volume caps.[4] In China, the central bank required central clearing of payment transactions by e-money providers, in part to make it easier for smaller e-money providers to compete with Big Tech firms (World Bank 2021a).

Big Tech companies will retain several inherent advantages even if they are subject to traditional regulatory requirements. Among others, they can leverage data from their nonfinancial operations,[5] which often have unique insights into customer behaviors and cash flows to which an incumbent bank would not have visibility. The value of this information is confirmed by the phenomenon of some Big Tech companies developing a credit score–like index and selling that information to third parties. The advantage over banks may be compounded where open banking forces incumbent financial institutions to share data with Big Tech firms, but there is no corresponding requirement on Big Tech firms to share their customer data.

Another source of advantage may come from product linkages and cross-subsidies. A Big Tech e-money issuer or digital bank could offer financial services at a steep discount because it expects to tap other revenue streams that would grow by offering financial services. For example, a Big Tech e-money issuer can generate revenue by offering advertising to a merchant and make the payment services free—a greater share of payment traffic will, in turn, help improve advertising offerings. An e-commerce marketplace can offer loans to merchants selling on its platform and make a margin on the increase in product sales as well as the loan.

Finally, the increased visibility and leverage over the client's activities may improve loan performance and collections. When sellers borrow from an e-commerce platform through which they sell to their customers, the loan repayments can be collected directly from their revenues, and they will be reluctant to default and risk being cut off from their customers. The differential in servicing costs and willingness to repay can manifest as lower costs of credit for the Big Tech firm relative to a bank.

Open banking. In 2018, the European Union and the United Kingdom led developments in regulation of open banking (World Bank 2022). Only three years later, several EMDE regulators have adopted or announced plans to launch similar initiatives. Significant diversity exists, however, in the motivations, scale, and scope of these initiatives.

In most countries, the regulations mandate that banks provide open APIs; in some others, open API provision is voluntary. Brazil developed a hybrid approach combining a mandatory provision to enable access to larger banks and conglomerates, while other financial institutions participate under a voluntary and customer-permissioned environment (World Bank 2022). The scope of the open banking regulations differs across jurisdictions. In Mexico, the regulations cover a wide range of institutions, including all financial institutions, but the scope of services is limited to information related to products and services and transaction inquiry; transaction initiation is not allowed as yet (World Bank 2022). Open banking regulations in other markets (whose frameworks are summarized in appendix D) cover a narrower range of institutions but enable a wider scope of activities.

Open banking was not necessarily designed with Big Tech firms in mind; however, they are likely to benefit significantly from it. The key motivation for open banking has been to foster competition and provide a pathway for fintech firms to offer services efficiently instead of having to rely on unreliable and risky processes like "screen scraping."[6] In some countries, the motivations have included facilitating greater adoption of digital approaches by enabling efficient, reliable data exchange. It is becoming clear that Big Tech firms, given their strong customer base and apps that are integrated into daily lives of end users, can derive significant benefits; for example, Google Pay dominates the third-party payment initiation market in India. See map 5.1 for a "heatmap" of global open banking implementations.

Looking Ahead

Different societies attach different preferences to market structure, and these preferences may evolve as countries climb the fintech adoption ladder. As such, authorities must be continuously intentional about outcomes. The "barbell" structure (as discussed in chapter 3)—or indeed other market structures that may emerge—may be more desirable or less desirable in a given market. The outcome will depend, among other things, on consumer behaviors and skills that determine switching costs in a given market and on how participants use their market power.

The impact of digital platforms that pursue growth over profits, and data over revenue, may not be well captured by competition policy approaches that focus on traditional measures of consumer welfare, such as costs and prices. Letting market forces determine the outcome may result in unexpected benefits or unwelcome consequences. For example, long-standing precepts on the separation of banking and commerce are already being upended. Prior approaches to the trade-offs between competition and stability, between inclusion and consumer protection, and between privacy and systemic integrity all must be reexamined. Fintech and

MAP 5.1 A Global Heatmap of Open Banking Implementation

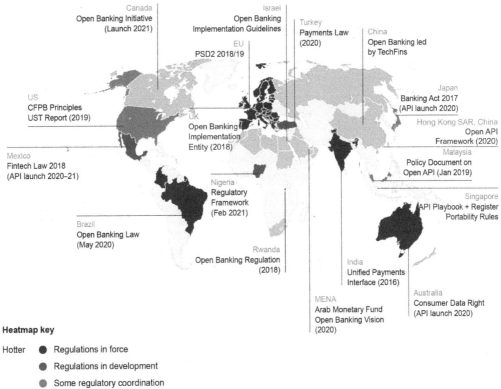

Canada
Open Banking Initiative
(Launch 2021)

Israel
Open Banking
Implementation Guidelines

Turkey
Payments Law
(2020)

China
Open Banking led
by TechFins

EU
PSD2 2018/19

US
CFPB Principles
UST Report (2019)

Japan
Banking Act 2017
(API launch 2020)

UK
Open Banking
Implementation
Entity (2018)

Hong Kong SAR, China
Open API
Framework (2020)

Mexico
Fintech Law 2018
(API launch 2020–21)

Malaysia
Policy Document on
Open API (Jan 2019)

Nigeria
Regulatory
Framework
(Feb 2021)

Singapore
API Playbook + Register
Portability Rules

Brazil
Open Banking Law
(May 2020)

Rwanda
Open Banking Regulation
(2018)

India
Unified Payments
Interface (2016)

Australia
Consumer Data Right
(API launch 2020)

MENA
Arab Monetary Fund
Open Banking Vision
(2020)

Heatmap key

Hotter   ●   Regulations in force

      ●   Regulations in development

      ●   Some regulatory coordination

Colder   ●   Industry and regulatory interest

Source: BBVA, findexable 2021.
Note: API = application programming interface; CFPB = US Consumer Financial Protection Bureau; EU = European Union; MENA = Middle East and North Africa; PSD2 = Payment System Directive 2; UK = United Kingdom; US = United States of America; UST = United States Treasury.

embedded finance may require not only the expansion of the regulatory perimeter but also an expanded perimeter of regulators: financial, consumer protection, competition, data/privacy, and telecommunications/internet.

Regulatory Implications

The implications of the cross-sectoral nature of fintech for regulation are profound. The boundaries between social networks, digital economy platforms, and financial services are blurring. Fintech- and Big Tech-embedded finance cut across financial supervisors, market conduct and competition authorities, and consumer protection agencies. As a result, regulatory approaches that separate commerce and banking may need to be revisited. Analyses of market concentration, use and abuse of monopoly power, and anticompetitive practices must take into account the economics of multisided platform models as well as the linkages of financial products to other activities where a single provider may have market power. New dynamics regarding both market structure and nonfinancial participants in payments and lending will require new thinking about systemic stability and monetary policy transmission.

Expanding the Regulatory Perimeter

The growing diversity of financial services providers and business models may require an expansion of the regulatory perimeter. Payments, loans, and deposit-taking services may be provided by specialized payment service providers (fintech firms), e-commerce platforms (Big Tech firms), and other nonbanks. Leaving activities outside the regulatory perimeter may entail risk. A lack of surveillance and oversight can hinder the regulators' ability to identify the relevant risks posed by a fintech activity early to avoid the accumulation of risks outside of the regulated perimeter. It is therefore important that regulators develop approaches to ensure a level playing field and provide clear requirements for licensing.

This blending of commercial and financial activity is not permitted under some financial regulation, resulting in a playing field that is not level. In Thailand, banks objected to e-commerce marketplaces being able to provide lending when banks were not allowed to provide nonfinancial products; in response, the regulator created space for banks to offer e-commerce marketplaces (Samalapa 2018). Indeed, the atomization and recombination of services enabled by connectivity and computing innovations blurs the borders of many economic sectors. One approach might be to regulate Big Tech firms as financial services providers. Such regulation might be feasible where there are payment services, insurance, or other specifically regulated activities. Credit is harder to regulate, since allowing a buyer to pay later is routine commercial practice. Some jurisdictions, such as Thailand, have looked instead to relax the restrictions separating banking and commerce.

New business models, particularly the ability to leverage data to manage risk, have also changed the balance of risks that drove the commerce-banking separation in the first place. In recent periods, financial services volatility has driven credit cycles more than real-sector volatility, so linking credit emission with real-sector activity might be stabilizing.

As a result, regulators are confronted with three critical questions: what to regulate, when to regulate, and how to regulate. The "what" pertains to which entities to bring within the regulatory perimeter. Once that is determined, the "when" question involves whether to intervene right away or to wait and see how the innovations shape up and whether they will pose risks. Some regulators have instead adopted an iterative approach—to "test and learn" by starting with some basic regulatory frameworks and observing the interplay of these with the market forces before developing a more detailed regulatory framework (Gispert et al. 2022). The recent developments of innovation facilitators, as discussed earlier in this chapter, provide a more structured way of implementing this approach.

The last part of the puzzle—on the "how"—could range from making marginal changes to existing rules based on traditional institution types to implementing a new customized fintech framework. In some cases, the existing framework will be fit for purpose or need only a few amendments. In other cases, the regulatory framework will need to be complemented by supplementary guidance. It may also be that the existing regulations are not directly applicable to the fintech activity but provide a solid basis from which to undertake the necessary changes to effectively regulate and supervise or allow a fintech activity. The Regulation technical note prepared for this publication (Gispert et al. 2022) describes a decision framework to navigate these three critical issues (figure 5.4).

The policy response chosen by each country will depend on the type of activity and country-specific factors, such as the stage of development of the financial sector, the size of the market, and the scale and type of fintech activity. Fintech activities that pose significant risks to the financial system will likely require authorization and a supervisory license to operate. The rest might only need to be registered with or notified to the relevant regulator.

The type of risks posed by the activity and its penetration will be the most relevant driver but not the only one. Country-specific factors include the state of the market, capacity constraints, existing financial regulatory frameworks, and the country's legal tradition. When the risks perceived are not high, EMDEs tend to allow fintech activity with no formal regulation. This approach may be related to the overall capacity and resource constraints that several of these countries face, the specific challenges posed by Big Tech firms (which offer a broader scope of services in EMDEs than in high-income economies), the often-underdeveloped state of fintech in the country, and lower competition levels in the financial service markets.

FIGURE 5.4 The Fintech Regulatory Decision Tree

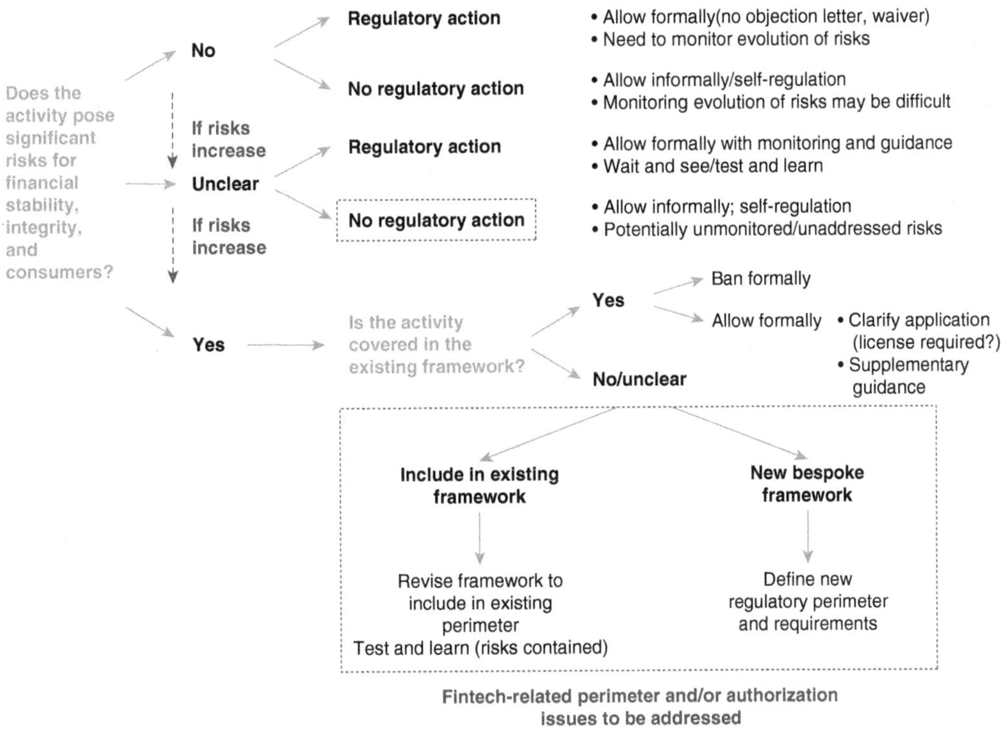

Source: Regulation technical note (Gispert et al. 2022).

Mitigating Risks Outside the Perimeter

Where the legal and regulatory changes to bring fintech entities and activities inside the regulatory perimeter may take time and may not be feasible, some fintech entities and activities may remain outside of the regulatory perimeter. In these circumstances, another mechanism to monitor risks is needed, such as a partnership with a regulated entity or a memorandum of understanding between the entity and the regulator. In some cases, fintech activities can be adequately monitored indirectly through their links with regulated entities within the regulatory perimeter. Such fintech activities usually fall under typical outsourcing constructs. However, even in such cases, authorities will need a way to monitor the collective impact on the financial system, which might be missed when monitoring indirectly.

In the absence of a competition mandate, financial sector regulators have several levers they can use to mitigate competition barriers and risks. They should understand the synergies and relationship between financial regulation and competition within their mandates. When establishing licensing frameworks, regulators may incorporate fair market entry aspects. They may also consider promoting a level playing field regarding distribution (agency banking and mobile money agents), data (open banking regimes), and customer due diligence (electronic Know Your Customer and tiered customer due diligence). Regulators could also ensure that financial infrastructures have fair and transparent access criteria that are the least restrictive and that any restrictions are justifiable on risk management grounds. Finally, financial regulators can collaborate with other authorities (for example, those overseeing telecommunications and other utilities that may offer financial services) as well as competition and data protection authorities.

Addressing consumer protection risks would require bringing fintech under existing consumer protection frameworks and addressing any gaps regarding specific risks that fintech can pose. Where no overarching consumer protection framework exists, customized conduct regulations could be an interim measure. Regulatory approaches to addressing such risks include

- Vetting of fintech entities during the authorization stage;

- Specifying risk management and governance obligations for platform operators;

- Imposing clear responsibility and liability on providers for the conduct of persons acting on their behalf;

- Placing targeted obligations on platform operators to safeguard consumers' interests regardless of business model (such as requiring peer-to-peer lending [P2PL] platform operators to undertake creditworthiness assessments, even if they are not themselves the lender);

- Providing warnings and other key disclosures to consumers regarding the risks associated with fintech products; and

- Segregating client funds.

Managing Digital Currencies and Crypto-Assets

The continued rise of new forms of digital money, such as central bank digital currencies (CBDCs) and crypto-assets, poses important issues. Many jurisdictions are contemplating the issuance of a CBDC. Although CBDCs could improve financial inclusion, efficiency, and cross-border payments, they are no panacea. Further, CBDCs may pose challenges related to data privacy and competition. They also consume significant resources to set up.

For their part, crypto-assets have been increasingly regarded and regulated as an emerging asset class. In light of sharp recent growth, some stablecoins could reach global scale quickly. Crypto-assets and stablecoins pose several public policy issues (box 5.2) and the potential for international regulatory arbitrage risks, requiring close international collaboration and guidance by standard-setting bodies within their respective mandates.

BOX 5.2

The Rise of Crypto-Assets and Stablecoins: Public Policy Implications

Although the impacts of crypto-assets and stablecoins currently remain limited, their adoption and use may evolve rapidly, calling for monitoring and continued progress on key policy considerations.

Monetary and fiscal issues. Given high price volatility and the current challenges to reach scale, crypto-assets appear to pose limited risks to monetary sovereignty. However, stablecoins, particularly those that operate at large scale and across borders, could pose issues to monetary policy transmission, lead to currency substitution, and affect capital flows in emerging markets and developing economies (EMDEs). Crypto-asset transactions that do not occur through regulated intermediaries may make it more difficult to identify tax evasion and enforce capital flow controls. Taxation on crypto-asset activity and capital gains could become a source of revenue.

Financial inclusion, cross-border payments, and remittances. Crypto-asset payment service providers have emerged that aim to enable near-instant, mobile-to-mobile small-value transactions at lower cost than existing solutions, using promising new open-source technologies (for example, the Lightning Network).[a] However, these technologies remain untested at scale and pose various risks that are not yet well understood. Moreover, many consumers' lack of access to smartphones and ID documents, as well as the need for physical access points, could make exchanges between physical fiat currency and crypto-assets difficult for the currently excluded customer segments.

Financial stability. As crypto-assets grow in size and interconnectedness with the financial system, they could have stability implications. These risks currently appear limited, but that could change rapidly. Stablecoins could pose issues related to financial stability and the smooth functioning of the payment system. In EMDEs, a lack of supporting domestic infrastructures, regulatory frameworks, and institutional capacity may complicate issues.

Illicit finance and market integrity. Crypto-assets pose such risks because of their decentralized and global nature. The Financial Action Task Force (FATF), in a recent 12-month review, finds the following: "The value of virtual assets involved in most [money laundering and

(Continued)

BOX 5.2
The Rise of Crypto-Assets and Stablecoins: Public Policy Implications *(continued)*

terrorist financing] cases detected to date remains relatively small compared to cases using more traditional financial services and products" (FATF 2021, 22). Industry estimates suggest that in 2021, illicit activity represented 0.15 percent of crypto-assets transaction volume, down from 3.4 percent in 2019 (Chainanalysis 2022).

However, crypto-assets have facilitated the rise in ransomware attacks. Many crypto-intermediaries are not registered or licensed, particularly in EMDEs, giving rise to regulatory arbitrage, data gaps, and issues regarding the safekeeping of users' assets, transparency of operations, price discovery mechanisms, and cyber resilience and security.

Investor and consumer protection. Most authorities have advised the public regarding the risks related to crypto-assets, such as their volatile nature. Unsophisticated users can easily have their funds lost or stolen with currently few, if any, redress options. Several projects also appear to be outright scams and frauds. Stablecoins aim to maintain a stable value relative to a reference asset; nevertheless they are subject to legal, exchange rate, and redemption risks and may raise antitrust issues if operated at large scale. These risks are exacerbated if intermediaries are not properly licensed and supervised, which makes enforcement of consumer and investor protection regulations difficult.

Energy consumption. Securing the value stored in crypto-assets networks and maintaining decentralization of the network requires energy. For example, Cambridge University estimates that Bitcoin, the largest crypto-asset, represents around 0.25 percent on average of global energy consumption.[b] A Cambridge Centre for Alternative Finance report estimates that 39 percent comes from renewable sources (Blandin et al. 2020). The industry is adopting more efficient hardware and exploiting "stranded" or nonrival sources of energy. In addition, many crypto-assets have emerged that do not use energy-intensive consensus mechanisms (for example, "proof of stake" instead of "proof of work").

a. The Lightning Network is a payment protocol layered on top of Bitcoin to enable real-time transfers (Lightning Network website: https://lightning.network/).
b. See the "Cambridge Bitcoin Electricity Consumption Index," Cambridge Centre for Alternative Finance, University of Cambridge: https://ccaf.io/cbeci/index.

Policy makers have hence taken a cautious stance regarding crypto-assets. Jurisdictions aim to provide an environment for safe innovation and adoption; they are clarifying existing or creating new legal, regulatory, and supervisory approaches, although some jurisdictions have limited or banned some or all crypto-assets activities. In light of their supranational and decentralized nature, crypto-assets pose international regulatory arbitrage risks. Various standard-setting bodies are applying general and transparent principles to provide guidance, set minimum requirements, and promote cross-border collaboration. In doing so, they must focus on economic functions and objectives, using a "same risk, same activity, same treatment" approach while aiming for simplicity, to ensure a future-proof, technology-neutral stance. However, this process remains a work in progress, and many national authorities still lag in upgrading their policy frameworks and addressing regulatory fragmentation.

Some types of crypto-assets, notably global stablecoins, have the potential to attract broad public use as a means of payments, including in the decentralized finance (DeFi) ecosystems. In this context, public authorities are actively exploring issuing CBDCs. Widespread adoption of crypto-assets could challenge the primacy of public money with implications for, among other things, monetary policy and financial stability. Some authorities have also noted the concentration and data protection and privacy risks that large-scale payment service providers can pose, particularly the ones employing a data monetization-led business strategy. It is perceived that a CBDC, being a digital version of fiat currency, could imbue public money with the necessary digital features and enable it to provide society with a safer, more efficient alternative while also promoting competition and innovation.

The perceived potential of CBDCs to advance financial inclusion is also of interest to some public authorities, notably in EMDEs. However, CBDCs are not a panacea for financial inclusion, because key behavioral, technological, and infrastructural barriers that are also faced by other digital payment solutions may remain in place. Further, alternative avenues to address the gaps that crypto-assets and CBDCs might seek to address—avenues such as implementing fast payment systems, enabling open banking, extending operating hours of payment systems, expanding membership of payment systems, and better integrating payment systems across the world—deserve equal attention.

Supervisory Implications

Countries will need to regularly evaluate the appropriateness of their supervisory frameworks to account for the digital transformation of the financial sector. Supervisory and regulatory frameworks are closely linked and influence each other. The supervisory framework should be well designed to respond to the risks inherent in fintech activities and flexible enough to adapt to rapid market developments. The framework should also embed proportionality to ensure that prompt supervisory actions are commensurate with the level of risk.

A single institutional model to supervise fintech activities is not necessarily feasible and, to date, no country has created one. Rather, supervisory responsibilities related to fintech tend to follow preexisting frameworks and mandates for financial sector supervision, although in some countries there is a debate on whether the existing framework and approach remains appropriate or whether adaptation and change is needed.

New Responsibilities, New Challenges

New responsibilities are being allocated to existing authorities. Because some services previously provided only by established financial institutions are now also provided by nonfinancial corporates and start-ups, questions arise as to which authority must supervise these. The contours of the regulatory perimeter have implications for supervision. The implications for supervision of activities outside the regulatory perimeter on regulated entities will also need to be assessed. In this regard, various fintech-specific supervisory challenges stand out.

Cyber risk and resilience. Cyber threats are bound to increase in an increasingly fintech-dominated financial sector, calling for prompt and timely supervisory action. International bodies and standard setters have issued guidance and stock takes—including the Group of Seven (G-7), the Basel Committee on Banking Supervision (BCBS), the Committee on Payments and Market Infrastructures and International Organization of Securities Commissions (CPMI-IOSCO), and the Financial Stability Board (FSB)—that outline supervisory requirements to mitigate cyber risks.

These risks typically involve (a) a documented cybersecurity program or policy; (b) identification of critical information assets; (c) testing; (d) cyber event reporting; (e) cyber threat intelligence sharing; (f) documented security capabilities of third-party service providers; and sometimes (g) security certification of information security professionals.

Reliance on third parties. As outsourcing by regulated financial institutions becomes more prevalent (and potentially systemic), supervisors are developing structured and proportional approaches that consider the materiality, complexity, and impact on business continuity. The outsourcing of critical services or functions would need prior authorization and to comply with requirements regarding data security, data protection and privacy, auditability, due diligence of providers, contingency plans, and reporting obligations. Cloud-based infrastructures raise unique concerns relating to outsourcing practices.

Data protection. Massive breaches of consumer data in recent years have left consumers vulnerable to identity theft and violation of their privacy. Data protection requirements are increasingly used in licensing frameworks. As such, supervisors will need to pay continuous attention to the disclosure of the types of data used by financial institutions. Supervisors must also pay attention to measures to help consumers understand how their data are being used as well as how to be able to grant or withdraw consent. Constraints on sending data across national borders are also increasingly applied.

Getting Up to Speed

Supervisors will need to catch up, particularly in EMDEs. To that end, supervisory agencies should regularly evaluate staff skills and gaps. Skills gaps typically include such areas as cybersecurity; legal matters (for example, to assess outsourcing contracts); data science and statistics (for example, to manage and extract insight from big regulatory data sets or to review models of financial institutions); and crypto-assets. In many EMDEs, supervisors are only starting to understand how fintech is affecting the financial sector, and they will need to strengthen institutional capacity, including by training existing staff and hiring new staff.

Authorities are embedding fintech skills into their organizations in different ways. Some authorities have established dedicated fintech teams that assist fintech firms with licensing issues and provide guidance throughout the process, including in innovation facilitators. Other authorities have embedded fintech expertise in traditional supervision units to promote cross-fertilization with financial sector and risk management disciplines. An intermediate option is to set up interdepartmental working groups that analyze the risks involved, the level of detail required by examinations, whether dedicated teams would be appropriate, and what specific expertise and techniques are required. Supervisory technology (regtech and suptech) approaches can facilitate supervisory and compliance processes for both the authorities and the industry and may help overcome resource constraints, but they are no panacea.

Effective supervision of fintech calls for coordination and information-sharing arrangements between domestic authorities. Fintech activities may fall within the regulatory perimeter of multiple agencies, but only a few jurisdictions have a formal body in charge of coordinating fintech policies. Collaboration mechanisms may be formalized through memorandums of understanding (MoUs) to cover cross-cutting issues—such as anti-money laundering and combating the financing of terrorism (AML/CFT) or consumer protection—with other financial sector regulators, including the national treasury, prudential authorities, the central bank, the financial sector conduct authority, telecommunications authorities, financial intelligence units, national credit regulators, and stock exchange authorities. The national or federal government might get involved in these MoUs when the impact transcends the financial sector, for example, in relation to digital ID, data privacy, or cybersecurity.

The practice of involving the industry in fintech coordination efforts in cybersecurity, payments, and securities is also becoming more frequent. Strengthening the engagement with the industry—such as by including regulatory sandboxes, accelerators, innovation hubs, and fintech coordination groups—provides excellent learning opportunities for supervisors to develop a deeper understanding of fintech and identify appropriate regulatory and supervisory responses.

International cooperation on fintech matters will further gain in importance, both bilaterally and in a multilateral context. In light of the cross-border and often global nature of fintech developments (for example, remittances, CBDCs, crypto-assets, cross-border payments, and cloud-service providers), authorities will need to strengthen coordination and information sharing to facilitate knowledge transfer and effectively monitor financial service provision that transcends jurisdictional boundaries. Initiatives to foster cooperation to agree on standards to develop suptech solutions that are compatible across countries are particularly necessary and valuable. The Global Financial Innovation Network (GFIN), an international network of more than 70 financial regulators launched in 2019, is a new model of international cooperation on fintech innovation and supervision that aims to increase collaboration between regulatory agencies in fintech and regtech.

Winding Down

The approach to dealing with fintech failures may need strengthening. Many jurisdictions have specific crisis management arrangements for regulated financial institutions, designed to preserve financial stability; the integrity of the financial sector; and the savings of depositors, investors, corporates, and households. For the most part, these regimes are not readily applicable to fintech firms. However, for fintech firms that work solely as intermediaries of transactions, the financial risks are limited and no special wind-down arrangements may be needed. This is the case, for example, for certain types of robo-advisors, which work like investment advisors. However, those that also handle client funds and execute the investment advice have the characteristics of brokers. Similarly, marketplace lending platforms might need to institute procedures ex ante to support the orderly termination, transfer, or continued servicing of loans and investments facilitated by the platform in case the platform exits the business. Moreover, authorities often impose requirements to ensure client access to relevant documentation and transaction data if these firms fail.

The basics of what to include in wind-down procedures are clear; however, there are challenges regarding legal basis and supervisory and operational capabilities. The procedures need to include an ex ante articulation of how customer positions and contracts can either continue to be operational or be transferred to another operator. However, there could be specific legal issues—starting from whether the regulators have the powers to require and administer these procedures to whether the underlying contracts or services are legally amenable to such procedures. Moreover, for these procedures to be credible, appropriate supervisory processes are needed to ascertain the effectiveness of the underlying arrangements and develop capabilities to operationalize these procedures.

E-money providers and other fintech firms that handle customer funds should adequately ring-fence their clients' funds and keep them segregated from the institution's own assets and in a safe place. Doing this will ensure that funds are readily available and easily transferable in case of failure, especially if they are kept in government securities or deposited with the central bank. In some cases, consideration could be given to extending the coverage of the deposit guarantee scheme to the balances of e-money accounts to protect customer funds against fraud or misappropriation of the reserves. Even so, without mechanisms to smoothly transfer balances to an alternative operator or servicer, customers may lose access for days or weeks, as was the case when Wirecard failed (Collins 2020).

Special wind-down procedures may be indicated where the fintech provider has systemic relevance. This could be the case, for example, in some markets where mobile money has been broadly adopted. Financial authorities must evaluate the potential impact of the failure of a systemically important fintech firm and address all major concerns appropriately. However, the lack of international standards or recommendations is a challenge, especially for EMDEs with capacity constraints.

Implications for Financial Infrastructure

Open access to payments infrastructures. Financial infrastructures that are available on terms typically associated with public goods—providing open, fair, and transparent access—are critical for market contestability. The Central Bank of Mexico, for example, is allowing nonbanks to access the payments infrastructure, and the Peoples Bank of China is allowing nonbank credit providers to access its credit registry. In other cases, regulators are requiring operators of financial infrastructures to open access to nonbanks. The Reserve Bank of India granted nonbank e-money issuers access to payments infrastructure. In some cases, new open infrastructures are being created—for example, in Pakistan and Sierra Leone—that would be open to all digital financial service players.

Interoperability and standardization. With new payment media emerging, including CBDCs and stablecoins, achieving interoperability and standardization of clearing and settlement rules and infrastructures will become critical. The Payments technical note prepared for this publication articulates that these features would allow users of different technologies or systems to interact with one another, improving their systems' effectiveness and efficiency (Delort and Garcia Luna 2022). This interoperability must be possible not only in terms of technology but also in terms of costs to avoid high charges derived from the interaction and transactions between systems.

Regulators can help to ensure a more seamless payments infrastructure and support interoperability, for example, by requiring market participants to develop end-user payment services based on open data-entry solutions to avoid the creation of closed payment solutions and fragmentation of the market. Governance of payment systems increasingly requires governments and regulators to be much more proactive in understanding, and, where needed, to set the standards for new technologies and business models and operating procedures and rules.

Central bank service modernization. The increasing role of fintech firms, adoption of fast payments, embedded finance, and cross-border financial flows will put pressure on central banks to modernize their settlement services. Options range from enhancements to existing systems to redesigning the provision of central bank money. Maintaining the status quo of restricting access to central bank settlement assets and services to only incumbents could amplify risks, hamper competition, reduce efficiency, and affect the safety and reliability of payment services.

For central banks, there are two nonexclusive sets of solutions: first, a more traditional response could be round-the-clock availability of settlement services, including expanding the range of entities that can access and embrace open APIs. Second, redesigning the provision of central bank money for a digital world, taking into account technological developments, could lead in the direction of CBDCs. The implications of the former are better understood than the latter.

Credit information sharing. The coverage, quality, and ease of accessing credit information reporting systems can enable new lenders and also preserve the soundness of incumbents. Whether credit information is assembled by an industry-led bureau or by a central bank registry, the core goal of preventing overindebtedness is thwarted if new lenders do not report credit exposures or lack access on an equal footing to existing credit exposure information.

At the same time, it should be recognized that inclusion-minded fintech firms may be lending to segments not currently covered by the bureau or registry. For example, in markets where there is no differential in pricing between an inquiry that returns information and a no-hit inquiry, to mandate that lenders must make bureau inquiries for all borrowers would impose excess cost on inclusive lenders trying to serve previously underserved market segments.

Recognizing that fintech business models often leverage alternative data, such as utility data or transactional data, the scope of credit information sharing might be expanded beyond lenders. Ideally, commercially beneficial arrangements can induce participation in credit information sharing, but they may need adjustments to the frameworks for information sharing to institutionalize the data subjects' control of their data and protect against unauthorized uses of personal data, algorithmic discrimination, and other abuses (Salamina et al. 2019).

Access to government data. The coverage, quality, and ease of access to government data can be a key enabler for fintech models. Fintech providers are required to conduct verification of their customers, conduct ongoing customer due diligence, and validate information on their customers and their assets. These processes benefit greatly from access to information held with public authorities, government agencies, and potentially other private sector players—for example, on ID, land records, demographic information, income tax records, education records, and employment history.

How fintech providers can access the data on customers held by the government—or by other providers—has an impact on their ability to serve their customers. Making these data available in an efficient manner using automated interfaces enables digital financial service providers to reduce their costs and improve customer convenience. In India, for example, automated access to government data platforms has enabled banks to approve micro, small, and medium enterprise (MSME) loans and personal loans online in under one hour, whereas it once took 20–25 days (Pazarbasioglu et al. 2020).

The big picture. The definition of infrastructure is broadening; technology brings in more players, and what constitutes infrastructure is becoming more fluid. As such, the challenges of *what* to regulate and *how* to regulate it become more challenging. On the one hand, new types of services like digital ID, alternative data, and orchestration of customer consent are becoming centralized and taking on characteristics of financial infrastructures. On the other hand, some financial service providers have become so dominant and have inserted themselves into the value chains of such a range of financial services that they are taking on some characteristics of financial infrastructure or quasi-infrastructure. How this new class of providers should be regulated to ensure protection of safety, reliability, competitiveness, and efficiency of the financial sector needs attention.

Financial infrastructure could be provided by entities in various corporate structures—for example, publicly owned, privately owned, for-profit, not-for-profit—and deployed in different technological approaches—centralized versus decentralized. Where private sector solutions do not emerge, public authorities may need to play a catalytic role, including potentially in building and operating necessary infrastructure. Irrespective of the form they take and the technology framework, certain key themes remain critical—prioritizing the needs of the overall ecosystem, safety, reliability, efficiency, sound risk management, and robust governance.

Notes

1. Both "emerging markets and developing economies" (EMDEs) and "advanced economies" are defined according to classifications of the International Monetary Fund's World Economic Outlook Database: https://www.imf.org/en/Publications/WEO/weo-database/2020/October/select-aggr-data.
2. These findings, from the 2019 Global Fintech Survey (IMF and World Bank 2019), categorized activities somewhat differently from those listed here.
3. For discussions of the European Commission's "Ethics Guidelines for Trustworthy AI" and the Monetary Authority of Singapore's fairness, ethics, accountability and transparency (FEAT) principles, see appendix E.
4. In March 2021, the National Payments Corporation of India (NCPI)—the umbrella entity for digital payments in India—issued "Standard Operating Procedure (SOP)–Market Share Cap for Third Party Application Providers (TPAP)." Under these guidelines, no single third-party application can exceed a market share of 30 percent by payments volume (NPCI 2021).
5. The use of such data could be by explicit consent of the customer, but a Big Tech company's customer would not have a similar capability to share the same information with a traditional incumbent bank.

6. "Screen scraping" is the process of using automated scripts to collect displayed data elements from one application so that the data can be used by another application (Mothibi and Rahulani 2020). Scraping from online platforms generally requires the use of customer credentials to log in and access the data as if the screen scraper was the customer.

References

Blandin, Apolline, Gina Peters, Yue Wu, Thomas Eisermann, Anton Dek, Sean Taylor, and Damaris Njoki. 2020. "3rd Global Cryptoasset Benchmarking Study." Report, Cambridge Centre for Alternative Finance, University of Cambridge.

Chainanalysis. 2022. "The 2022 Crypto Crime Report." Annual data and research report, Chainanalysis, New York.

Collins, Barry. 2020. "Customers Left with No Money as Wirecard Fallout Continues." *Forbes*, July 2.

Delort, Dorothee, and Jose Antonio Garcia Garcia Luna. 2022. "Innovation in Payments: Opportunities and Challenges for EMDEs." Payments technical note for *Fintech and the Future of Finance*, World Bank Group, Washington, DC.

Didier, Tatiana, Erik Feyen, Ruth Llovet Montañés, and Oya Ardic. 2022. "Global Patterns of Fintech Activity and Enabling Factors." Fintech Activity technical note for *Fintech and the Future of Finance*, World Bank, Washington, DC.

FATF (Financial Action Task Force). 2021. "Second 12-Month Review of the Revised FATF Standards on Virtual Assets and Virtual Asset Service Providers." Report, FATF, Paris.

Feyen, Erik, Harish Natarajan, Guillermo Galicia Rabadan, Robert Paul Heffernan, Matthew Saal, and Arpita Sarkar. 2022. "World Bank Group Global Market Survey: Digital Technology and the Future of Finance." *Fintech and the Future of Finance* technical note, World Bank, Washington, DC.

Gispert, Tatiana Alonso, Pierre-Laurent Chatain, Karl Driessen, Danilo Palermo, and Ariadne Plaitakis. 2022. "Regulation and Supervision of Fintech: Considerations for EMDE Policymakers." Regulation technical note for *Fintech and the Future of Finance*, World Bank, Washington, DC.

IMF (International Monetary Fund) and World Bank. 2019. "Fintech: The Experience So Far." Policy Paper No. 2019/024, IMF and World Bank, Washington, DC.

Mothibi, Kagiso, and Awelani Rahulani. 2020. "Non-Traditional Research Data Report 2020." Report, Financial Sector Conduct Authority, Pretoria, South Africa.

NPCI (National Payments Corporation of India). 2021. "Standard Operating Procedure (SOP) – Market Share Cap for Third Party Application Providers (TPAP)." Circular, NPCI, March.

Pazarbasioglu, Ceyla, Alfonso Garcia Mora, Mahesh Uttamchandani, Harish Natarajan, Erik Feyen, and Mathew Saal. 2020. "Digital Financial Services." White paper, World Bank, Washington, DC.

Salamina, Luz Maria, Pratibha Chhabra, Shalini Sankaranarayan, and Collen Masunda. 2019. "Disruptive Technologies in the Credit Information Sharing Industry: Developments and Implications." Fintech Note No. 3, World Bank, Washington, DC.

Samalapa, Patchara. 2018. "E-Marketplace Set to Heat Up as Mobile Banking Gains Ground." *The Nation Thailand*, February 25.

Vigdor, Neil. 2019. "Apple Card Investigated after Gender Discrimination Complaints." *New York Times*, November 10.

World Bank. 2021a. "Developing Digital Payment Services in the Middle East and North Africa: A Strategic Approach." Report, World Bank, Washington, DC.

World Bank. 2021b. *World Development Report 2021: Data for Better Lives.* Washington, DC: World Bank.

World Bank. 2022. "Technical Note on Open Banking: Comparative Study on Regulatory Approaches." Report of the Financial Inclusion Global Initiative, World Bank, Washington, DC.

CHAPTER 6

Conclusion

Emerging Policy Implications

The ongoing transformation of finance represents a paradigm shift. It calls for new approaches to regulation and supervision as well as heightened collaboration and cooperation with other public authorities across issues affecting data protection, privacy, and competition. Financial sector and other public authorities will need to step up to this challenge to play a critical role in fostering sound fintech adoption and the development of responsible, open, and inclusive markets for digital finance. In this regard, several policy implications emerge.

1. Foster beneficial innovation and competition while managing the risks. In light of the fast-evolving landscape and rapid spread of innovations from market to market, adopting an enabling approach to support responsible fintech innovation and adoption is critical. Authorities must be proactive, pragmatic, clear, and collaborative with public and private stakeholders to promote trust, innovation, and investment, particularly since fintech issues cut across financial prudential supervisors, market conduct and competition authorities, and consumer protection agencies.

2. Be mindful of evolving policy trade-offs as fintech adoption deepens. One size will not fit all. For example, the prudential and monetary policy implications of digital money and alternative credit at low levels of penetration are different from those at higher levels. Policy trade-offs will evolve as fintech continues to permeate the financial and nonfinancial sectors. These developments will call for proper safeguards to ensure fair competition, maintain financial stability, ensure data and consumer protection, and prevent the abuse of market power.

Seek to balance the inherent trade-offs among policy options within a complex market environment as fintech adoption reaches scale. Areas where issues of stability, competition, concentration, efficiency, and inclusion may need to be reweighed include

- Data collection principles and proactive monitoring of market conduct;

- Frameworks for open banking and data ownership;

- Development of financial infrastructures and fair and transparent access to them; and

- Restrictions on activities such as product tying and linkages between banking and commerce.

3. Broaden the horizons for monitoring, and reassess regulatory perimeters as embedding of financial services blurs the boundaries of the financial sector. Financial services are increasingly provided by a wide variety of entities, making services more decentralized, often embedded into other products and services, and frequently delivered as part of commercial transactions or social interactions underlying customers' workflows and daily activities. Drivers of these trends include the atomization of financial services value chains, the unbundling of products, and separation of customer interfaces from underlying accounts.

These trends are leading to a more complex constellation of traditional regulated institutions, technology companies, fintechs, consumer Big Tech firms, and others creating the firmament of financial services. The solutions they offer can deliver efficiency, greater inclusion, and improved development outcomes where they are responsibly adopted. However, the variety of providers raises questions on the scope and intensity of regulation and supervision: Which of these institutions and services should be monitored or regulated? How can the monitoring entities calibrate supervisory intensity? Developing the ability to monitor the entire financial sector value chain and to reshape the regulatory perimeter is therefore essential.

4. Review regulatory, supervisory, and oversight frameworks to ensure that they remain fit for purpose and enable the authorities to foster a safe, efficient, and inclusive financial system. The range of new products and providers, use of new technologies and a wider range of data, and inclusion of new customer segments in increasingly complex markets is making existing regulatory and supervisory mandates and approaches insufficient, risking fragmentation of the institutional landscape. The decentralization of financial services as embodied in crypto-assets also poses domestic and international regulatory arbitrage challenges, and countries should adopt new binding global standards as quickly as possible. Broad principles that help underpin the policy stance include

- Ensuring an approach that is proportional to risks;

- Maintaining a level playing field by treating the same activities and same risks similarly, looking past the specific technologies chosen (technology neutrality); and

- Ensuring the primacy of core policy objectives, which may call for customized approaches.

5. Anticipate market structure tendencies and proactively shape them to foster competition and contestability in the financial sector. While the initial focus has been on facilitating entry, and the momentum of innovation has been from small start-ups and new entrants, the market is already rapidly boomeranging toward concentration of players and platforms, especially due to economies of scale and network effects in data. That trajectory may deliver inclusion and efficiency, particularly in low- and middle-income economies that lack a robust, competitive, and inclusive banking sector. Regulators will need to proactively monitor market conduct and ensure that markets remain at least contestable while continuing to dynamically balance trade-offs between competition, concentration, efficiency, data protection, and inclusion.

6. Modernize and open up financial infrastructures to enable competition and contestability. Financial infrastructures should be interoperable and open to both new and traditional players (for example, through open application programming interfaces [APIs]) to promote network effects, innovation, and competition. The increasing role of fintech companies, embedded finance by Big Tech companies, digital money, and cross-border financial flows will put pressure on regulators to ensure that financial infrastructures have fair and transparent access policies that are not used to lock out competition. This is particularly critical when the financial infrastructures are owned by incumbents.

The governance arrangements of financial infrastructures will become an important element for regulators to monitor and shape. Moreover, with the entry of new market-level services that take on the characteristics of financial infrastructures, regulators will need to assess whether and how to bring them within the regulatory perimeter.

7. Ensure that public money remains fit for the digital world amid rapid advances in private money solutions. Crowding out of public money will hamper the ability of public authorities to shape and safeguard financial sector and economic development. The ongoing developments in the digitization of the economy and payments, the world of crypto-assets, and the influence of Big Tech firms in payments and user data could, over time, challenge the role of public money, competition, and privacy.

In addition to strengthening policy frameworks regarding crypto-assets and Big Tech firms, as well as modernizing and opening up payments and related market infrastructures, public authorities might need to consider structural alternatives like central bank digital currencies (CBDCs). Countries that consider launching a CBDC should carefully evaluate the wide-ranging implications and design options in consultation with public and private stakeholders.

8. Pursue strong cross-border coordination and sharing of information and best practices, given the supranational nature of fintech. Fintech developments enable providers to reach a wide set of customers across borders and provide services without necessarily being subject to regulation in the customers' jurisdictions. Regulators and public authorities will need to collaborate and coordinate with their peers to safeguard their respective financial systems and customers. In this regard, global standard-setting bodies and international bodies like the International Monetary Fund and the World Bank have a critical role.

Final Remarks

This list has attempted to capture key areas of policy considerations, but is perforce limited by both space and time. The specific needs of individual markets and economies will vary, and the list can only reflect what has been observed, and what can be inferred for the future, at a particular point in time. Even as these lines are being written in November 2022, the bankruptcy of a major crypto-asset exchange and the talk of a "crypto winter" portends renewed debate on approaches toward regulating that sector (Cecchetti and Schoenholtz 2022; Krugman 2022).

Looking to underlying technology drivers and economic forces can help policy makers focus their efforts on responding to fundamental changes in financial services rather than to specific product innovations. For example, peer-to-peer lending (P2PL) was an early product innovation leveraging the ability to connect multiple lenders to a single borrower and to construct a loan from diversified funders without deposit intermediation. The P2PL wave has subsided, but the fundamental changes it represented—including de-linking deposits from lending and mimicking intermediation products with something that looks similar but significantly shifts the risks (in this case, to individual investors holding slices of a direct loan)—will endure.

Addressing these changes comprehensively within any regulatory framework will be a continuous challenge as markets endlessly innovate and evolve. This volume has tried to make the case for the positive opportunities presented by financial innovation—for economic efficiency, inclusion, and development—while acknowledging the risks and identifying paths for their mitigation and oversight. At the end of the day, however, no attempt to evaluate the opportunities against the risks is needed. Only the most closed of markets can avoid innovation, which will wait for no regulator. There is no choice, then, but for policy itself to innovate and play its role in shaping the future of finance.

References

Cecchetti, Stephen, and Stephen Schoenholtz. 2022. "Let Crypto Burn: Just Say No to Legitimacy-Inferring Regulation." *Financial Times*, November 17. https://www.ft.com/content/ac058ede-80cb-4aa6-8394-941443eec7e3.

Krugman, Paul, 2022. "Is This the End Game for Crypto?" *New York Times*, November 17. https://www.nytimes.com/2022/11/17/opinion/crypto-banks -regulation-ftx.html.

Overview of Recent Market Developments

Fintech Activity Index

The Fintech Activity Note prepared for this report develops a novel country-level index of fintech activity for 125 countries covering 2014–2018 (Didier et al. 2022). The index covers three dimensions of fintech activity: (a) fintech firm creation and growth through the availability of early-stage equity financing; (b) use of fintech credit and digital payments, currently the most commonly used digital financial services, especially in low- and middle-income countries; and (c) use of mobile distribution channels for financial services.

Fintech activity is closely associated with information and communication technology (ICT) infrastructures and financial sector development in several respects (Didier et al. 2022):

- *ICT infrastructure.* Fintech activity is positively associated with ICT and financial infrastructures, though the relevance of the specific type of infrastructure varies across types of fintech services. Specifically, the evidence indicates that payments infrastructure plays a more important role in the use of digital payment services, whereas the development of credit information systems is more relevant to the use of digital lending services.

- *Banking.* There is a robust negative association between fintech activity and bank development, consistent with the view that digital financial services may have more opportunities to develop in countries where the underserved and unserved shares of the market are relatively large. Countries with more stringent overall banking regulations exhibit subdued fintech activity, suggesting that this is linked to a less permissive environment for innovation and fintech entrants. At the same time, bank app downloads are more prevalent in countries with more stringent banking regulations, suggesting in these cases that the digital transformation is driven by incumbents.

- *Capital markets.* Fintech activity is positively correlated with capital market development. This association suggests that a supportive funding environment for fintech firms, especially start-up equity financing, can play an important role.

Many of the first round of consumer fintech firms were unbundling plays, offering a single product or a few tightly integrated solutions. Examples include mobile wallets, product search and comparison apps, peer-to-peer (P2P) lending, remittance or international transfer, and stock trading apps, as well as business-to-business (B2B) solutions offering processing efficiencies, data analytics, or other services to established players. Some of these were regulated, such as payments and remittances, or worked with regulated institutions, for example, to book loans via a bank partner if required in their jurisdictions. Others were in unregulated spaces or were outright regulatory arbitrages, such as P2P lending; the category definer, Zopa, was designed specifically to avoid being categorized as a deposit taker.

Despite the advantages of not requiring physical infrastructure and scalable technology, fintech strategies have boomeranged toward rebundling and even licensed banking. Increasingly, one-time, single-product firms that avoided the regulated space are seeking licenses, in some cases because regulators have closed loopholes and limited arbitrage opportunities. Customer acquisition, regulatory requirements, and building trust (including investments in brand recognition) introduce costs that can only be justified with a higher lifetime customer value—which can only be achieved with a broader range of products. This is particularly true for fintech lenders that obtained banking licenses to access low-cost deposit funding. Once the overhead of a bank license has been incurred, a single-product strategy no longer makes sense. There is an observable trend of fintech firms seeking banking licenses and of new fintech firms entering the market as licensed neobanks.

Payments

Payments are probably the financial activity most affected by innovation and have undergone radical changes from various perspectives. This transformation—prompted by the adoption of new technologies and business models, the emergence of new market players, and changes in the structure of the market—is having a profound impact beyond the realm of payments by also affecting the real economy. Significant changes include the following:

- Once a supporting function offered typically only by banks as part of a bundle of services and with comfortable profit margins, payments have become a stand-alone product. In other words, they have become a separate, identifiable service offered by a growing number of providers, including nonbanks, exercising a downward pressure on fees and margins as well as an upward demand for quality.

- The consumer experience has been transformed to overcome long-standing barriers or frictions that had deterred the use of digital payments and also to meet new demands from payers and payees for increased speed and convenience and lower prices.

- In some cases, like in ride-hailing or meal-ordering apps or in "one-click" online ordering, the purchase experience has been totally transformed by making the payment process "invisible" from the customer's perspective.

- Payments are increasingly becoming a source and provider of data that are critical for differentiation against competitors and for the provision of other products and services, including but not limited to those offered by financial sector entities.

- Innovation in payments has also enabled and shaped up major developments in the real economy such as the surge of e-commerce—including transactional online services offered by governments—and in turn new platform models, which have put additional demands on payment services.

Although innovation in the area of retail payments has been prolific, it has not fully transmitted to specific payment streams like international remittances and other forms of cross-border payments, some types of government payments, and B2B payments.[1] For example, the Committee on Payments and Market Infrastructures (CPMI) reports that cross-border payments lag domestic payments in terms of cost, speed, access, and transparency (CPMI 2020).

In the area of government payments, many emerging markets and developing economies (EMDEs) still have a long way to go in digitizing their payments and collections effectively, largely because of coordination challenges and other elements that slow down the generalized use of payment innovations. In this area, however, the COVID-19 crisis has favored an acceleration of these digitization efforts—for example, to facilitate the transfer of relief funds while at the same time trying to ensure social distancing.

As for B2B payments, this market segment has certain unique requirements like the linkage to invoicing processes and taxation, and payments tend to be for larger amounts. To date, these unique requirements have not been fully met.

Credit

The available data suggest that digital credit has grown significantly, driven by Big Tech firms most recently (Cornelli et al. 2020). According to Bank for International Settlements (BIS) credit statistics, in 2019, total credit to the nonfinancial sector from banks and other intermediaries was around US$185 trillion globally and US$60 trillion in EMDEs. Cornelli et al. (2021) document that, in 2018, credit provided by fintech firms had grown to an estimated US$296 billion globally. However, China, one of the leaders in fintech credit growth, imposed regulatory restrictions, resulting in a global decline in fintech credit to US$167 billion in 2019. Fintech lending continued to grow outside of China in 2018–19, but the overall volume was lower owing to the decline in China.

In 2020, the biggest portion of the global decline was again in China, where fintech lending all but ceased with the closure of P2P platforms. Fintech credit volumes also fell during the COVID-19 pandemic in some other key jurisdictions, including India, the Republic of Korea, the Netherlands, and the United Kingdom. However, volumes rose in the United States, where fintech platforms were able to participate in the federal government's Paycheck Protection Program, through which certain businesses and organizations received loans to continue paying their workers.[2] Meanwhile, credit provided by Big Tech firms reached US$700 billion in 2020 and is growing fast in Asia and some countries in Africa and Latin America. (See also the section below on "Platform Models and Embedded Finance.")

Digital credit is driven by several supply and demand factors. Cornelli et al. (2020) find that both fintech and Big Tech credit tend to be higher in countries where gross domestic product (GDP) per capita is higher, banking systems are less competitive, fewer regulatory restrictions are in place, the ease of doing business is greater, and investor protection disclosure and the efficiency of the judicial system are more advanced. Fintech credit is also inversely related to bank branch concentration. They conclude that fintech and Big Tech credit are complementary to, rather than substitutes for, traditional forms of credit provision.

There are still sizable data gaps on digital credit provision. Many fintech credit providers, such as P2P and marketplace lending platforms, are not (yet) regulated and therefore not subject to regular reporting requirements. In addition, standard reporting requirements for more established, regulated financial institutions are not well suited to separately capturing their provision of digital financial services. For instance, it is hard to identify digitally originated loans extended by banks or the extent to which their loan underwriting and processing has migrated toward newer technologies.

Digital credit can help expand coverage to those with limited access to traditional sources of bank credit. For example, MYbank, an online bank serving micro and small enterprises in China, uses e-commerce and digital payments data from Alibaba and Alipay and adaptable scoring and risk management to lend to small companies, many of which have limited access to bank finance. Research on lending to 2 million firms that borrowed from MYbank and from traditional banks between 2017 and 2019 found that MYbank's underwriting was less dependent on the financial cycle (World Bank 2022). MYbank expanded its customer base and also partnered with 118 other banks to leverage MYbank's transaction data, automated processing, and risk management to lend to SMEs as they resumed operations (MYbank 2021).

Recent analytical work around credit during the COVID-19 pandemic recovery has pointed to the importance of fintech firms and other digitally enabled lenders for economic resilience (World Bank 2022). While traditional credit data became less useful during the pandemic—since credit histories did not reflect the pandemic's impact on a borrower's finances—alternative data such as real-time transactions data from payments, inventory orders, and sales provide more visibility to current activity and cash flows. Fintech lenders and embedded finance providers with access to more timely data were well positioned to lend into the uncertainties of the pandemic and the recovery phase. For example, Konfio, a Mexican fintech lender, adapted its credit algorithm to integrate data on the sectoral impacts of COVID-19 containment measures (Cantú and Ulloa 2020). The company was able to limit portfolio delinquencies and recalibrate underwriting to resume lending to both existing and first-time clients, growing new loan bookings from August 2020 onward and fully recovering prepandemic monthly disbursement levels by early 2021.

Remittances

The Fintech Activity Note shows that technology can help reduce the costs associated with remittances on which many households in EMDEs rely (Didier et al. 2022). Remittances are small-value, cross-border, person-to-person transfers (CPMI and World Bank 2007). They are an essential source of income for millions of families across EMDEs. When regulators and policy makers create the right enabling environment, remittance service providers can leverage new technologies for the benefit of migrants and their families back home—for example, in the form of cost and time savings.[3] At the same time, the use of technology can help reduce the time it takes to transfer funds. This includes time spent for travel and wait times.

Mobile money for international remittance transfers can lower fees for sending remittances. The Global System for Mobile Communications Association (GSMA) notes that the use of mobile technology reduces the cost of remittances by half (GSMA 2016, 2018). Based on the Remittance Prices Worldwide (RPW) database, the World Bank reports that as of the fourth quarter of 2020, the global average cost for digital remittances was recorded at 5.11 percent of the total amount sent, while the global average cost for nondigital remittances was 6.99 percent.[4]

The speed of an international remittance transaction is another challenge for which innovative models can provide solutions. International remittances take longer to process from end to end than domestic transfers for a variety of reasons, including differences in daily cutoff times and closing times in different jurisdictions as well as the time required for reconciliations, dispute resolutions, and anti-money laundering and combating the financing of terrorism (AML/CFT) checks to name a few. New technologies can offer innovative ways to overcome lengthy procedures for these purposes. The analysis shows that a larger share of services offered by digital money transfer operators is associated with lower average costs.[5]

Crypto-Assets and Decentralized Finance

Technology is gradually blurring one of the last functional boundaries—the distinction between an individual and a financial intermediary. In a future of increased connectivity and decentralized finance (DeFi), individuals may play hybrid roles or even directly provide financial services. For example, if search and contracting costs are sufficiently reduced, an individual with savings to deploy need not place the deposit at a bank but instead can lend money directly to one or more borrowers.

Distributed ledger technology (DLT) has already demonstrated the potential to transfer value without intermediaries. P2P marketplaces have demonstrated the feasibility, and the risks, of direct lending. Various platforms are developing blockchain-native assets that will enable investments without brokers or exchanges. The pieces are falling into place to enable intermediary-free finance to develop as another stream of financial services.

Crypto-Assets and Related Developments

Crypto-assets operate on open, decentralized networks that enable users to store, transfer, and receive funds with global reach without the need for financial intermediaries. In this context, crypto-assets have put a welcome spotlight on some deficiencies in the financial and monetary system. Some of these deficiencies are related to financial inclusion, financial literacy, public trust in traditional financial intermediaries, cross-border payments and remittances, and macroeconomic policies.

The adoption of crypto-assets in EMDEs appears higher in countries with weaker macroeconomic and financial conditions and infrastructures, giving the impression to some that crypto-assets could fulfill an important role if conventional alternatives are lacking or perceived as riskier and where trust in public institutions and the financial sector is lacking. Crypto-assets face various technical challenges to reach scale, although the industry is attempting to overcome them through new technologies.

Crypto-assets have been increasingly regarded and regulated as an emerging asset class.[6] The Digital Money technical note prepared for this publication argues that most crypto-assets are currently volatile and often considered an investment asset rather than a medium of exchange or store of value (Feyen et al. 2022a). The market value of crypto-assets exhibited various boom-bust cycles, reaching an all-time high of US$2.8 trillion in November 2021. Some industry estimates suggest that 100–200 million people around the world own or use crypto-assets. A Statista household survey found that there are at least 20 countries where over 10 percent of the respondents owned or used crypto-assets in 2021, many of which are EMDEs.[7] Several large banks, payment card companies, and payment processors have started to offer crypto-asset services.

Decentralized finance. Some crypto-asset platforms also allow for a complex, interoperable ecosystem of financial services to emerge, called decentralized finance (DeFi). These platforms can run decentralized applications that offer a range of interoperable financial services such as exchange, trading, collateralized lending, borrowing, escrow, derivatives, and the creation of new crypto-assets with user-designed properties, all seemingly without the need for intermediaries or governing bodies that exert significant control.[8] Developers can use these services as building blocks to create new services.

This unintermediated form of finance would render any individual with surplus funds a financial services provider. The emergence of individuals as direct providers of financial services is nascent at present, but it cannot be discounted as a potential influence on market structure in the future. DLT that underpins crypto-assets may have applications beyond finance, including for digital identification (ID), data exchange, and providing users with control over their own data.

Stablecoins. In response to the high volatility of crypto-assets, "stablecoins" have emerged as a new type of crypto-asset. No stablecoin that operates at large scale globally is currently operational. Stablecoins attempt to maintain a stable value relative to a fiat currency or a basket of fiat currencies or other reference assets. Some stablecoins, such as now-defunct Facebook's Diem (formerly Libra), may tap into large existing user bases of social media and e-commerce platforms, thus reaching global scale quickly. The Group of Seven (G7) determined that "A global stablecoin for retail purposes could provide for faster and cheaper remittances, spur competition in payment services and thus lower costs, and support greater financial inclusion" (Coeuré 2019).

Central Bank Digital Currencies

These developments have prompted central banks and public authorities to evaluate the issuance of digital variants of fiat currency—central bank digital currencies (CBDCs)—because a large-scale shift to crypto-assets or stablecoins would have implications for, among other things, financial stability and monetary sovereignty. CBDCs, unlike crypto-assets and stablecoins, would be a liability of the central bank and be a digital variant of fiat currency—and as such, being legal tender, would be freely convertible to notes and coins and commercial bank money at par.

Central banks and international bodies are actively deliberating on different design options for CBDCs, and the discussions thus far categorize CBDCs in several ways (World Bank 2021):

- By who has access (wholesale versus retail)

- By whether there is an underlying account (account-based versus token versus DLT account)

- In the case of retail CBDCs, by who manages the customer relationship (Tier 1, as when the central bank manages the relationship, versus Tier 2, when licensed financial institutions manage the customer relationships)

- By scope of use (domestic versus cross-border).

To date, The Bahamas, the Eastern Caribbean Central Bank, and Nigeria have launched retail CBDCs that are account-based, using a two-tiered design and restricted to domestic use. China is conducting live testing on a retail CBDC and has made the same design choices. Several other countries, including Ghana and Jamaica, are in advanced stages of issuing retail CBDCs. Although CBDCs need not be built on decentralized architectures, they could nevertheless have a role in supporting the functioning of the DeFi services and provide an alternative to stablecoins and crypto-assets.

Cross-border payments service providers have emerged that use open-source technologies built on top of Bitcoin (that is, the Lightning Network). These providers aim to enable near-instant, mobile-to-mobile-based, small-value transactions, perhaps at lower cost than existing solutions, using promising new technologies. However, these technologies remain largely untested in a real-world environment at scale. Moreover, these services may raise various issues including liquidity, operational issues, consumer protection, and money laundering and terrorist financing risks.

Transformation of Incumbents and B2B Services

Incumbent financial institutions have also adopted new technologies and reconfigured their production of financial services to improve efficiency and compete with new entrants. The Fintech Market Participants Survey conducted for this publication found that digital transformation is a strategic priority for the overwhelming majority of incumbents, to shed overhead costs and employees, improve products, and compete for consumer relationships (Feyen et al. 2022b). The COVID-19 pandemic increased the urgency of these efforts.

Large banks tended to be ahead of smaller banks and to feel that digital transformation was affecting their businesses positively. This might be expected, given the resources required to take full advantage of digitization across channels, products, and processes.

The divergence of banks by size also maps to divergences across countries. Banks in EMDEs tend to face significant resource constraints. In particular, the skills required for digital transformation are in short supply in many emerging markets. Indeed, the Fintech Market Participants Survey responses confirmed that EMDE banks were less positive than those in high-income economies about how fintech and digital transformation were affecting their businesses (Feyen et al. 2022b). This is also consistent with the Fintech Activity Note's observation that there is a negative association between fintech activity and bank development, meaning banks in EMDEs may be facing more competition from fintech firms (Didier et al. 2022).

Digitization of channels and process is under way. Fintech Market Participants Survey respondents expected digital sales and customer origination to shift from predominantly 0–25 percent in 2019 (figure A.1, panel a) to higher shares within five years (figure A.1, panel b). Similarly, internal processes are expected to be significantly digitized. However, half of banks and remittance operators, and 60 percent of microfinance institutions, nonbank financial institutions (NBFIs), and payments operators expected business to continue to be conducted largely through physical locations (Feyen et al. 2022b). Nevertheless, banks expected to continue serving customers through their own delivery channels while other providers look to more diverse channels and partners.

In pursuing their own digital transformations, incumbents have become important consumers of B2B fintech and Big Tech services. These include cloud-based services provided by Big Tech firms to banks as well as fintech service components (for example, loan servicing) that banks incorporate into their product offerings. There is a growing trend of banks and fintech firms cooperating to white-label or codeliver fintech products; these partnerships enable (a) the bank to short-cut its internal innovation cycles to deliver services to its customers, and (b) the fintech to leverage an existing customer base at reduced acquisition costs.

Incumbents also continue to have a comparative advantage in managing complex balance sheets and regulatory compliance; as a result, many fintech and Big Tech firms work with banks to offer financial services. This is often necessary for consumer-facing (B2C) fintech and Big Tech firms to access the regulated financial system—for example, to execute real-time payments. Depending on a fintech firm's business model and the local regulatory environment, customers may need to have a financial institution account to hold funds, or the tech company may have to hold all customer funds in a bank trust account. The unbundling of payments, use of application programming interfaces (APIs), and open banking enables regulated banks to turn this into a business model, offering banking as a service (BaaS) to enable nonbank providers to "rent" licensed capabilities such as holding deposits or providing balance-sheet capacity, linkage to payments infrastructure, and compliance services. The fintech

FIGURE A.1 **Use of Digital Channels for Sales and Customer Origination**

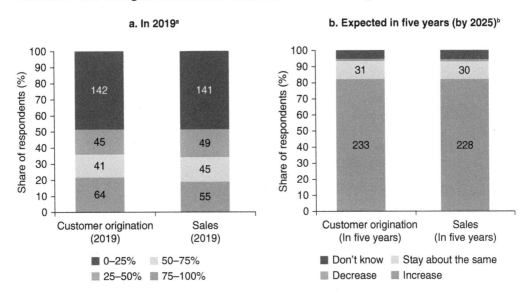

a. In 2019[a]

b. Expected in five years (by 2025)[b]

Source: Feyen et al. 2022b.

Note: The chart shows the distribution of responses to questions on the use of digital channels and processes in the World Bank's survey, conducted May 2020 to January 2021, of 330 fintech market participants from 109 countries. Responses have been aggregated across product lines and responding institution type. Numbers within the bars represent the number of respondents in relation to the shares of respondents (aligned with y-axis values). Respondents represented traditional banks, payments and remittance service providers, fintech firms, insurance companies, nonbanking companies, technology companies, telecommunications companies, industry associations, and other financial market players. The total number of responses per question varied. Responses of "No response" or "No answer" are excluded from the chart. For more information, see Feyen et al. (2022b) or the summary in appendix B.

a. Respondents answered the following multiple-choice questions (panel a): "What proportion of your new customers originate through digital channels today? What proportion of your sales originate through digital channels today?" Answer choices were 0–25 percent, 25–50 percent, 50–75 percent, and 75–100 percent.

b. Respondents answered the following multiple-choice questions (panel b): "What proportion of your new customers will originate through digital channels in five years? What proportion of your sales will originate through digital channels in five years?" Answer choices were "Increase," "Decrease," "Stay about the same," and "Don't know."

firm can then focus on customer experience and service and avoid having to obtain a license.

Financial Infrastructure Operators

In addition to banks, incumbent financial infrastructure operators are also deeply impacted by the ongoing changes. This is especially the case for international and domestic payment card networks and Automated Clearing House (ACH) service providers. The Payments technical note produced for this report observes that the business strategy of payment card networks and ACHs is evolving as they attempt to reinvent themselves and their business model along several key paths (Delort and Garcia Luna 2022):

- They try to become themselves operators of fast payment services.

- They evolve into gateways and hubs for open banking and API-based services.

- They position themselves as payment systems underpinning CBDCs, stablecoins, and crypto-assets.

- They introduce services for B2B payments, like direct corporate access in ACHs and by adding services on top of existing card rails to carry the additional B2B information.

- The international card networks in particular are becoming white-label service providers for some cross-border payment services like remittances. Similarly, credit-reporting infrastructures are foraying into provision of value-added services integrating alternative data, providing digital ID services, and becoming hubs for open banking.

Credit information systems are also transforming. Bureaus and registries are upgrading their infrastructure to handle new participants and larger volumes. They are increasingly adding alternative data to expand their coverage, for example, by collecting utilities payment histories, which may include more individuals than have had prior access to a bank loan.

At the same time, the proliferation of credit-relevant data other than traditional credit histories has fostered the entry of new credit information and credit-scoring providers. Some of these, for example, analyze telecommunications data and social media footprints to create a credit score. Others use transaction data from financial services, utilities, and other sources. By one tally, there are 246 alternative data credit-scoring providers globally.[9]

Platform Models and Embedded Finance

Scale and scope economies, along with network effects, play to the fundamental strengths of Big Tech companies. They have established customer bases, extensive customer data, and unique positioning to provide contextual finance. Platforms and other tech players can reduce customer acquisition costs and leverage data for marketing and risk management, especially where they are mediating the underlying business transaction for which a financial service is required. More importantly, they can leverage their position as a business facilitator to enforce good behavior and can potentially cross-subsidize the financial service from other income.

Early platform forays into financial services were in payments, filling a gap in the online market. eBay bought PayPal because there was no card-acquiring business serving the individuals and small merchants trading on its platform; offering payments was necessary to grow the marketplace business. The same was true for Alibaba's introduction of Alipay and the development of wallets by ride-hailing firms such as Grab and Gojek in Southeast Asia. Having met a need within their platforms, these payments businesses did not always charge for their services since the platform derived income from the core business transaction that was being facilitated. Eventually they found traction and created synergies across a broader set of use cases.

Payment services are increasingly seen as services distinct from provision of an underlying transaction or credit account. This has enabled different trajectories for embedded payments, as exemplified by Amazon Pay, which executes Amazon customers' payments for other e-commerce sites. Amazon itself is the merchant of record, working with a merchant acquirer to accept card payments, and most users in its core markets have credit or debit cards. Executing payments for Amazon sellers became another part of the overall marketplace offering. Providing Amazon Pay to other websites and online sellers[10] is a reflection of Amazon's market dominance—as if to say, "Your customer is probably already an Amazon user, so we have his or her payments information"—as well as consumer preferences for convenience and privacy.

Platforms and Big Tech firms are increasingly offering credit to their users, directly or via partners. A common use case is providing working capital for merchants selling through e-commerce platforms. Because the platform has extensive information about the merchant's prior sales, fulfillment record, customer satisfaction, and other data, it is in a position to predict cash flows and ability to repay. And because it also is handling the merchant's revenues, it can take repayment for a loan out of future sales through the platform. In some cases, this embedded lending is done by the platform itself and in other cases through partnerships with fintech lenders or banks. Another instance of embedded finance is buy-now-pay-later funding for consumers, which leverages the selling website's customer acquisition and data.

SME Finance

One important market segment that is benefiting from the digital transformation of finance (and of commerce more broadly) is the small and medium enterprise (SME) sector. Fintech can help address key barriers SMEs face in access to finance, particularly in EMDEs: high cost to serve; lack of credit history or collateral; and bankability, both in terms of registration, verification, and record keeping and in terms of financial literacy and capacity (Teima et al. 2022). As an example of the potential regarding cost to serve, 90 percent of banks responding to the Fintech Market Participants Survey expect digital transformation to reduce costs of SME lending (Feyen et al. 2022b).

New entrants (fintech and Big Tech firms) are driving tailored customer-centric products and processes as well as new business models that can compete with traditional players on price, convenience, and inclusivity. Banks and NBFIs are adopting new technology to compete, sometimes in partnership with fintech firms. A bank that successfully deploys technology to serve its customers better and more profitably will have lower unit costs and lower cost of capital as well as more data to fine-tune its algorithms, further reducing its credit costs. From the perspective of SMEs, new entrants offering tailored, focused products and large players improving their efficiency and pricing by leveraging technology all help improve access to finance.

To realize this potential, economies need adequate digital infrastructure, regulatory frameworks supportive of digital onboarding, new providers, and both innovative products and capacity building for SMEs. Promoting broad-based digitization of SME activities would not only improve entrepreneurs' efficiency and access to markets but also reinforce improvements in SME registration and identity verification and create a foundation of business data that can used for financing.

Notes

1. There have been also some relevant developments in large-value payments, which have been less visible for those not specialized in the payments space as well as for the general population. These include the adoption of the International Organization for Standardization (ISO) multipart ISO 20022 message standards, cloud-based hosting of payment solutions, and expanding access to large-value payment systems to participants other than banks.

2. Ziegler et al. (2021) refer to fintech lending as "debt-based alternative finance."

3. According to the World Bank's Remittance Prices Worldwide (RPW) database, the speed of an international remittance transaction varies by the type of the remittance service provider: the average speed of a transaction is 25 hours, but it is close to five days (69 hours) for banks and less than one day (17 hours) for nonbanks.

4. Fourth-quarter 2020 remittances data are from the RPW database: https://remittanceprices.worldbank.org/. These costs are reported as the average costs of sending US$200. A digital remittance must be sent via a payment instrument in an online or self-assisted manner, and received into a transaction account, that is, a bank account, transaction account maintained at a nonbank deposit-taking institution (say a post office), or mobile money or e-money account.

5. The analysis uses data from the World Bank's RPW database: https://remittanceprices.worldbank.org/.

6. Crypto-assets are broadly defined as digital representations of value that can be used for payment or investment purposes or to access a good or service and rely on open-source distributed ledger technology (DLT) or similar technology through the internet. A distributed ledger is often referred to as a "blockchain" (see Glossary).

7. "Share of respondents who indicated they either owned or used cryptocurrencies in 56 countries and territories worldwide from 2019 to 2022," Statista Research Department data (published October 4, 2022): https://www.statista.com/statistics/1202468/global-cryptocurrency-ownership/.

8. See, for example, Harvey, Ramachandran, and Santoro (2021) and Schär (2021).

9. "Top Alternative Credit Score Providers Startups," Tracxn (updated October 13, 2022), https://tracxn.com/d/trending-themes/Startups-in-Alternative-Credit-Score-Providers.

10. "Let Amazon Customers Pay Their Preferred Way without Ever Leaving Your Site," Amazon Pay website, https://pages.amazonpayments.com/Amazon-Pay-for-merchants.html.

References

Cantú, Carlos, and Bárbara Ulloa. 2020. "The Dawn of Fintech in Latin America: Landscape, Prospects and Challenges." BIS Paper No. 112, Bank for International Settlements, Basel, Switzerland.

Coeuré, Benoit. 2019. "Update from the Chair of the G7 Working Group on Stablecoins." Speech to the G7 Finance Ministers and Central Bank Governors Meeting, Chantilly, France, July 18.

Cornelli, Giulio, Sebastian Doerr, Lavinia Franco, and Jon Frost. 2021. "Funding for Fintechs: Patterns and Drivers." *BIS Quarterly Review* (September 2021): 31–43.

Cornelli, Giulio, Jon Frost, Leonardo Gambacorta, Raghavendra Rau, Robert Wardrop, and Tania Ziegler. 2020. "Fintech and Big Tech Credit: A New Database." Working Paper No. 887, Bank for International Settlements, Basel, Switzerland.

CPMI (Committee on Payments and Market Infrastructures). 2020. *Enhancing Cross-Border Payments: Building Blocks of a Global Roadmap.* Basel: Bank for International Settlements.

CPMI (Committee on Payments and Market Infrastructures) and World Bank. 2007. *General Principles for International Remittance Services.* Basel: CPMI, Bank for International Settlements; Washington, DC: World Bank.

Delort, Dorothee, and Jose Antonio Garcia Garcia Luna. 2022. "Innovation in Payments: Opportunities and Challenges for EMDEs." Payments Note for *Fintech and the Future of Finance*, World Bank, Washington, DC.

Didier, Tatiana, Erik Feyen, Ruth Llovet Montanes, and Oya Ardic. 2022. "Global Patterns of Fintech Activity and Enabling Factors." Fintech Activity Note for *Fintech and the Future of Finance*, World Bank, Washington, DC.

Feyen, Erik, Jon Frost, Harish Natarajan, and Tara Rice. 2022a. "What Does Digital Money Mean for Emerging Market and Developing Economies?" Digital Money Note for *Fintech and the Future of Finance*, World Bank, Washington, DC.

Feyen, Erik, Harish Natarajan, Guillermo Galicia Rabadan, Robert Paul Heffernan, Matthew Saal, and Arpita Sarkar. 2022b. "World Bank Group Global Market Survey: Digital Technology and the Future of Finance." Fintech Market Participants Survey for *Fintech and the Future of Finance*, World Bank, Washington, DC.

GSMA (Global System for Mobile Communications Association). 2016. "State of the Industry Report on Mobile Money, Decade Edition: 2006–2016." GSMA, London.

GSMA (Global System for Mobile Communications Association). 2018. "State of the Industry Report on Mobile Money 2018." GSMA, London.

Harvey, Campbell R., Ashwin Ramachandran, and Joey Santoro. 2021. *DeFi and the Future of Finance.* Hoboken, NJ: John Wiley & Sons.

MYbank. 2021. "MYbank Aims to Bring Inclusive Financial Services to 2,000 Rural Counties by 2025." Press release, April 30.

Schär, Fabian. 2021. "Decentralized Finance: On Blockchain- and Smart Contract-Based Financial Markets." *Federal Reserve Bank of St. Louis Review* 103 (2): 15374.

Teima, Ghada, Ivor Istuk, Luis Maldonado, Miguel Soriano, and John Wilson. 2022. "Fintech and SME Finance: Expanding Responsible Access." SME Note for *Fintech and the Future of Finance*, World Bank, Washington, DC.

World Bank. 2021. "Central Bank Digital Currency: A Payments Perspective." Guidance note, World Bank, Washington, DC.

World Bank. 2022. *World Development Report 2022: Finance for an Equitable Recovery.* Washington, DC: World Bank.

Ziegler, Tania, Rotem Shneor, Karsten Wenzlaff, Krishnamurthy Suresh, Felipe Ferri de Camargo Paes, Leyla Mammadova, Charles Wanga, Tania Ziegler, Rotem Shneor, Karsten Wenzlaff, Krishnamurthy Suresh, Felipe Ferri de Camargo Paes, Leyla Mammadova, Charles Wanga, Neha Kekre, Stanley Mutinda, Britney Wanxin Wang, Cecilia López Closs, Bryan Zhang, Hannah Forbes, Erika Soki, Nafis Alam, and Chris Knaup. 2021. "The 2nd Global Alternative Market Benchmarking Report." Report, Cambridge Centre for Alternative Finance, Judge Business School, University of Cambridge.

Executive Summaries of Technical Notes

Data Trends and Market Perceptions

Global Patterns of Fintech Activity and Enabling Factors (Fintech Activity Note) by Tatiana Didier, Erik Feyen, Ruth Llovet Montanes, and Oya Ardic

The objectives of this note are to take stock of the available fintech-related data, to document patterns of fintech activity across the world, and to help identify enabling factors. Fintech has seen remarkable growth over the past few years and will likely continue to shape the financial sector in terms of products, business models, and industrial organization. Yet measurement of fintech activity is challenging, complicated by both the lack of a widely accepted definition and important data limitations.

Methodology

This note tackles this measurement challenge by leveraging a wide range of data sources and developing a novel, country-level index of fintech activity for 125 countries, covering 2014–18. The index covers three dimensions of fintech activity: (a) fintech firm creation and growth through the availability of early-stage equity financing; (b) use of fintech credit and digital payments, now the most commonly used digital financial services, especially in low- and middle-income countries; and (c) use of mobile distribution channels for financial services.[1]

The fintech activity index is positively correlated with countries' overall level of economic development. For instance, high-income countries generally rank higher than middle- and low-income countries not only in terms of the aggregate fintech index but also along its three constituent dimensions. However, significant variation across both regions and income groups persists, suggesting that other enabling factors matter.

This note then uses the index to systematically analyze the association between fintech activity and a wide range of economic and technological factors in a multivariate regression setting. Specifically, the paper explores the role of three broad sets of enabling factors:

- *Basic foundations,* including information and communication technology (ICT) and financial infrastructures

- *Financial sector development,* distinguishing between the development of the banking system and capital markets

- *The enabling policy environment,* capturing the legal and regulatory frameworks for digital financial services.

Key Findings

Basic foundations. First, the estimations show that fintech activity is positively associated with ICT and financial infrastructures, though the relevance of the latter varies across types of fintech services. Specifically, the evidence indicates that the ICT payments infrastructure plays a more important role in the use of digital payment services, whereas the development of credit information systems, a financial infrastructure, is more relevant for the use of digital lending services.

Financial sector development. Second, the analyses also show a robust negative association between fintech activity and bank development, consistent with the view that digital financial services may have more opportunities to develop in countries where the underserved and unserved shares of the market are relatively large. Countries with more stringent overall banking regulations exhibit subdued fintech activity, suggesting that this is linked to a less permissive environment for innovation and fintech entrants. At the same time, bank app downloads are more prevalent in countries with more stringent banking regulations, suggesting in these cases that the digital transformation is driven by incumbents.

Importantly, the estimations also show that fintech activity is positively correlated with capital market development. These correlations stem from the development of digital financial services by institutions other than banks, such as fintech companies. The positive association with capital market development suggests that a supportive funding environment for fintech firms, especially start-up equity financing, can play an important role. For example, the mobile app data show that downloads of nonbanking apps are significantly positively related to the development of capital markets but negatively associated with banking system development. The opposite patterns are observed for bank app downloads. The analysis thus supports the idea that the distinction between incumbent banks and fintech companies is particularly important when exploring the potential drivers of fintech activity.

The enabling policy environment. Third, the empirical results are consistent with a high-quality policy environment as a necessary but insufficient condition for fintech development. Other factors must be in place as well for fintech activity to flourish. The degree of fintech activity is consistently on the low end of the distribution in countries scoring poorly on policy indexes that capture the existence of legal and regulatory frameworks relevant for digital financial services, but it varies widely across countries scoring high on these indexes. In fact, several countries exhibit relatively low levels of fintech activity despite having a supportive enabling policy environment. Finally, regulation could have a positive and stabilizing impact on fintech activity in the longer term. These benefits are not likely to be reflected in the analysis, given the relatively short time horizon.

Regarding the role of sector-specific legislation and regulations, the results show mixed patterns. Although the existence of laws and regulations for e-money, digital identification, e-signatures, and electronic Know Your Customer (eKYC) frameworks tends to be positively associated with fintech activity, the coefficient on consumer protection tends to be negative. The results, however, are not as forceful as those related to the other set of enabling factors and may reflect the complexities of policy interactions, preconditions, and trade-offs at different levels of fintech development as well as measurement challenges. Moreover, it is important to recognize that alternative policy combinations can promote innovation and foster fintech activity, with similar outcomes.

Overall, the demands on the enabling environment will likely evolve as fintech activity develops. Finding the right balance between trade-offs at every stage of fintech development remains essential to promote activity and innovation while keeping excessive risks in check.

Additional analyses. Finally, separate in-depth analyses documented in the appendixes of the Fintech Activity Note explore two additional topics: the impact of the COVID-19 pandemic on finance app downloads and the link between the digitization of remittances services and remittance costs. On the former, the paper's analysis of mobile app download trends indicates that the pandemic may have accelerated fintech adoption. Moreover, the evidence indicates that the strict social distancing practices, including government-implemented containment measures such as lockdowns, quarantines, and travel restrictions required to mitigate the spread of the coronavirus, have amplified the use of digital financial services.

As for the link between the digitization of remittances services and remittance costs, the results indicate that digital service providers may help lower the costs of cross-border remittances, a key financial service for households in many emerging markets and developing economies. Specifically, the analysis shows that remittances costs are lower in corridors with a higher prevalence of digital service providers.

World Bank Group Global Market Survey: Digital Technology and the Future of Finance (Fintech Market Participants Survey) by Erik Feyen, Harish Natarajan, Robert Paul Heffernan, Matthew Saal, and Arpita Sarkar

Digital technologies have made an indelible impact on the provision of financial services by new entrants and incumbents alike. The World Bank conducted a global survey on fintech and digital transformation of a range of financial market participants. The survey sought to capture market perceptions of the impact of fintech and digital technology on the following:

- *Market developments,* including the impacts, risks, and benefits of fintech and digital transformation

- *Evolution of consumer behavior,* including consumer relationships with traditional and new financial service providers as well as consumers' use of physical locations

- *Competition and market structure,* including the perceived risk of losing customers, risks to profitability, potential to reduce costs, market concentration, competition, and outsourcing

- *Corporate strategy,* including priorities at the board level, strategic fintech activities, challenges to digital transformation, and the impact of COVID-19 on strategic priorities

- *Regulatory environments,* including the enabling environment for innovation for incumbents and new entrants as well as whether regulatory framework and guidance are fit for purpose in key product areas.

Survey Participants

From May 2020 to February 2021, 330 market participants from 109 countries responded to the survey. These included representatives of traditional banks, payments or remittance service providers, fintech firms, insurance companies,[2] nonbanking companies, tech companies, telecommunications companies, industry associations, and other financial market players from countries in all six World Bank Group regions. The survey was updated to include questions on the impacts of the COVID-19 pandemic.

Key Findings and Takeaways

Consistent with other surveys conducted by the World Bank Group, International Monetary Fund, and the Cambridge Centre for Alternative Finance, fintech and digital transformation, accelerated by the pandemic, was expected to increase in importance. This trend was largely welcomed by respondents[3] and seen as positive for financial services businesses. Key strategic priorities for firms included digitization of customer acquisition and account opening, creating new digital products, and transforming internal processes. More than 80 percent of respondents felt that the COVID-19 pandemic increased the need for fintech and digital transformation and made digitization in customer channels, product adaptation, and internal processes a strategic priority.

There were differing expectations, often by type of respondent, on channels and customer preferences. Reduced entry barriers were expected to increase competition, yet except for nonbank financial institutions (NBFIs), most respondents expected markets to become more concentrated. Respondents were concerned about increases in operational and cyber risks as a result of fintech and digital transformation. The regulatory framework and guidance for fintech and digital transformation innovation could be improved, particularly regarding remote onboarding and account opening, use of agents or third-party channels, and automation of new products.

This note is organized as follows: Section 1 provides background on the survey's objective. Section 2 summarizes the demographics of survey respondents.

Section 3 presents survey findings, organized according to the key topics covered by the questionnaire, from digitization trends to evolving customer needs to provider views on risk and regulation. Section 4 synthesizes this analysis and highlights six key themes that emerge, as described below.

Digital transformation of financial services was pervasive, strategically imperative, and was accelerated by the COVID-19 pandemic. Eighty-two percent of all respondents across all types of institutions expected an increase in the digital proportion of key activities. Fintech and digital transformation were strategic priorities at the boardroom level for 82 percent of respondents. More than 70 percent of respondents indicated that the pandemic increased the need for digital transformation across customer channels, internal processes, and product adaption. Respondents expected digitization to deliver significant benefits to customers and the firms themselves.

The future combines physical and digital—"phygital"—aspects. Digitization does not spell the end of physical infrastructure for financial services. Half of banks and remittance operators and 60 percent of microfinance institutions, NBFIs, and payments operators expected business to be conducted largely through physical locations in the next five years. Banks expected to continue serving customers through branches and proprietary digital channels, while other providers looked to more diverse channels and partners.

Customer relationships are changing, and incumbents and new entrants perceived customer relationship preferences very differently. Who will "own" the consumer relationship is in flux, as is how the customer will be served. There were strong expectations that new types of providers—neobanks, fintech firms, Big Tech firms, platforms, and aggregators—will dominate customer relationships. Even as banks continued to expect customers to have a single core relationship for their financial services, only 34 percent expected that to be with traditional banks.

Banks and fintech firms did not see each other as competitors. Respondents tended to see the greatest competitive threat coming from institutions that are similar to them. Banks mostly saw other banks and neobanks as a bigger competitive threat than other fintech players. Fintech firms expected to compete with other new types of players such as Big Tech firms, platforms, or aggregators. While there may be distinct customer segments, given the broader ambitions of neobanks, fintech firms, and incumbents, they cannot all be correct about what the majority of customers prefer.

Most financial services will be more competitive but also more concentrated. Forty-eight percent of respondents believed that competition will increase and that barriers to entry will lower to a great degree, while another 40 percent believed that this will happen to a moderate degree. Except for NBFIs, most respondents expected markets to also become more concentrated. This is consistent with a bifurcated market in which lower barriers to entry increases competition for smaller players or in specific segments such as those where NBFIs mainly operate, while economies of scale and network effects drive consolidation among large multiproduct institutions such as big banks, larger fintech firms, and Big Techs.

Regulatory and supervisory barriers to innovation need attention. While the regulatory stance with respect to enabling innovation was seen as "about right" by a majority of respondents, in 9 out of 12 specific areas, the regulatory framework and guidance was seen as lacking (that is, less than 60 percent of respondents agreed that it is fit for purpose).

Fintech and the Digital Transformation of Financial Services: Implications for Market Structure and Public Policy (Market Structure note) by Erik Feyen, Jon Frost, Leonardo Gambacorta, Harish Natarajan, and Matthew Saal

Financial intermediaries, such as banks and insurance companies, act as the middleman, linking participants in financial transactions. Economic frictions in the form of information asymmetries and economic forces, such as economies of scale and scope, give rise to financial intermediaries and shape financial markets. While technological advances are not new to finance, digital innovation has brought major improvements in connectivity of systems, in computing power and cost, and in newly created and usable data. This digital innovation is shaking up financial intermediaries and the markets in which they operate.

Market Implications and Outcomes

Digital improvements have alleviated transaction costs and given rise to new business models and new entrants. As technology has increased information exchange and reduced transaction costs, the production of financial services could be disaggregated. Specialized players have unbundled financial services, allowing consumers to find and assemble their preferred suites of products.

Digital technologies are reshaping payments, lending, insurance, and wealth management—a process that the COVID-19 pandemic has accelerated. Although these developments are making financial services in many economies more diverse, competitive, efficient, and inclusive, they may also increase concentration in markets. Economies of scale and scope as well as network effects are present in many aspects of financial services production, including customer acquisition, funding, compliance activities, data, and capital (including trust capital). Despite advances in technology, the costs of consumer search and assembly remain significant. These forces encourage rebundling and confer advantages to large multiproduct providers, including technology (Big Tech) firms expanding into financial services from adjacent markets.

Moreover, new risks may arise to a range of key public policy goals. This note draws on the underlying economics of financial services and their industrial organization to examine—with recent empirical evidence—the implications of digital innovation for market structure and attendant policies, including financial and competition regulation.

The organizing framework for the discussion is built around how economic frictions and economic forces, mentioned above, are driving market changes. For example, mobile phone use has surged globally; social and economic activity has shifted online, often to platform-based businesses; and new technologies like cloud computing have been widely adopted.

These improvements have alleviated frictions, blurred firm and industry boundaries, and given rise to new business models. New and often smaller and more specialized financial technology (fintech) players have unbundled services. Economies of scale and network effects are strong in digital platforms and cloud computing. These scale effects, alongside economies of scope, encourage rebundling and allow large technology (Big Tech) firms and other new players to deepen inroads into core financial product markets. Available evidence shows that Big Tech firms are rapidly expanding their footprint in finance and can use Big Data in ways that reduce the need for collateral. Meanwhile, incumbent financial institutions have adapted by adopting new technologies and by disaggregating their production of financial services to improve efficiency.

Digital innovation could drive a range of industrial organization outcomes. On the one hand, digital technology enables niche providers to reach a target customer base and be economically viable. On the other, customer acquisition, funding, "assembly," and switching costs tend to favor larger providers. One possibility is a "barbell"-shaped market, composed of a few large players and many niche players. The large, multiproduct players could include traditional financial institutions, fintech firms, and Big Tech firms—both incumbents and new entrants. Small players may include product-, geographic-, or sector-focused fintech firms and incumbents.

Although a barbell market is not the only potential outcome, it is a central case given the economic forces at work. It is a potential steady-state market structure as some participants leverage scale economies and network effects to grow larger while innovation continues to result in new entrants. Market forces will push players to either hyperfocus or aim for the large, multiproduct type of service offering. However, atomization—the reduction of services to their most basic parts—may continue and reaggregation could stall, leading to a market of more small players. Then again, limits on entry could result in a completely different market configuration. It's difficult to predict.

Policy Implications

This analysis gives rise to important policy issues regarding competition, regulatory perimeters, and how to ensure a level playing field. Concentration risks may increase in the provision of financial services to end users, and in the provision of infrastructure to financial institutions. Market structures that concentrate data and supercharge network effects could reduce intermediation costs and broaden inclusion. In many markets, however, the resulting market power might be detrimental. Competition regulators will have to strike a balance appropriate to the needs of their markets, since different societies will attach different preferences to market structure outcomes.

At the same time, financial regulatory authorities are working to manage policy trade-offs between stability and integrity, competition and efficiency, and consumer protection and privacy. The barbell outcome, for example, could present challenges to stability regarding both large and small payers. Widespread access to data raises privacy concerns. Regulators need to balance the innovation and efficiency brought by new entrants with the potential challenges for oversight, enforcement, and consumer protection. Emerging policy approaches—such as new antitrust rules for the digital era, data mobility requirements, and data protection laws—may help mitigate the policy trade-offs. Yet the responsibility for these changes generally lies with different public authorities as well as with legislatures.

Financial services are undergoing a profound transformation. To navigate this new territory effectively, and to balance the necessary policy goals, authorities will need to collaborate. This must occur both domestically—with cooperation between central banks, financial sector regulators, other industry regulators, and competition and data protection authorities—and across borders.

Such collaboration can help to ensure regulatory consistency and peer learning within and between countries as well as, ultimately, better development outcomes for the country.

Regulation and Supervision of Fintech: Considerations for EMDE Policymakers (Regulation Note) by Tatiana Alonso Gispert, Pierre-Laurent Chatain, Karl Driessen, Danilo Palermo, and Ariadne Plaitakis, with contributions from Ana M. Carjaval and Matei Dohotaru

Fintech is transforming the global financial landscape. It is creating new opportunities to advance financial inclusion and development in emerging markets and developing economies (EMDEs) but also presents risks that require updated supervision policy frameworks. Fintech encompasses new financial digital products and services enabled by new technologies and policies (BIS 2019). Although technology has long played a key role in finance, recent fintech developments are generating disruptive innovation in data collection, processing, and analytics. They are helping to introduce new relationship models and distribution channels that challenge traditional ways of finance while creating additional risks.

Although most of these risks are not new, their effects and the way they materialize and spread across the system are not yet fully understood, posing new challenges to regulators and supervisors. For example, operational risk, especially cyber risk, is amplified as increasing numbers of customers access the financial network on a 24/7 basis. Likewise, increased reliance by financial firms on third parties for provision of digital services, such as cloud computing, may lead to new forms of systemic risks and concentration on newly dominant, unregulated players such as Big Tech firms.[4]

Objectives of the Note

This note aims to provide EMDE regulators and supervisors with high-level guidance on how to approach the regulating and supervising of fintech, and more specific advice on a few topics. Preserving the stability, safety, and integrity of the financial system requires increased attention to competition, to ensuring a level playing field, and to emerging data privacy risks. As a general principle, a policy response should be proportionate to the risks posed by the fintech activity and its provider. While striking the right balance can be challenging in the absence of global standards, the Bali Fintech Agenda (IMF and World Bank 2018), along with guidance by standard-setting bodies, provides a good framework for reference.

Key Messages

A sound policy design must start with assessment of the fintech landscape, its risks, and regulatory gaps. Simplicity and pragmatism—for example, combining simple regulations with supervisory judgment—increases the odds of successful policy. In practice, this will mean different things, depending on the local context. In many cases, a clarification or review of existing frameworks will be sufficient and is easily done through enhanced supervisory guidance. In others, a full regulatory overhaul might be required. In some systems, an activities-based, technology-neutral approach based on the function of the financial service can help balance stability and innovation goals. In others, a combined approach, taking into account the activity and the entity, might be necessary to ensure financial stability. In any case, there needs to be clear definition of which activities are under the regulatory perimeter and which requirements apply, including the need for licenses. Some fintech activities will require licenses with integrity (anti–money laundering and combating the financing of terrorism [AML/CFT]) and conduct requirements. The introduction of data protection provisions in licensing frameworks is common. Activities that could potentially pose risks to stability should face prudential requirements.

Competition and inclusion objectives will become more relevant from a financial policy view, given the growing interdependencies and trade-offs with core priority mandates of preserving stability, integrity, and safety of the financial sector. The multiplicity of new entrants and the potential for dominant players (for example, incumbents, Big Techs, platforms) and first movers (for example, M-Pesa) to create barriers and generate distortions has led to an increased recognition of the strong links between inclusion, competition, and financial stability. Indeed, targeted participation by financial service authorities in competition policy matters is increasingly being observed in EMDEs. The importance of the potential role of prudential and conduct regulation in mitigating barriers to market access and reining in abusive dominant practices should not be understated.

Cooperation, both interagency and cross-border, can help in the design and implementation of a sound supervisory response to fintech, which can be particularly challenging for EMDE countries suffering from supervisory capacity constraints or juggling competing policy priorities. An effective supervisory function for fintech activities is as essential as an appropriate regulatory regime. Supervisory processes and methods may need significant changes. Supervisors' knowledge, skills, and tools should keep pace with the speed of innovation and related risks, including cyber threats. Building proper expertise is crucial, and supervisory technology (suptech) and regulatory technology (regtech) solutions could be excellent catalysts for this.

Fintech is cross-sectoral and cross-country, making cooperation among agencies at the national and international levels essential for sound supervision. Although many supervisors in Group of Twenty (G-20) EMDEs participate in international forums, smaller jurisdictions may need to rely on international financial institutions and other available channels—for example, the Global Financial Innovation Network (GFIN)—to raise issues, keep abreast of global developments, and exchange best practices. Involving the industry in fintech policy coordination efforts in a responsible and transparent way also appears increasingly relevant in areas such as cybersecurity, data, payments, and securities as well as for the design and implementation of regtech and suptech solutions (Appaya et al. 2020).

Further, authorities must ensure that client funds are well preserved and that proper wind-down mechanisms are in place for systemically relevant firms operating in fintech. For crisis management, fintech providers should be treated the same as their peers in traditional finance. For e-money institutions (EMIs) and payment institutions, regardless of their size, mechanisms should be established to require adequate ring-fencing of client funds and proper segregation, preferably by keeping them in government securities or deposited with the central banks.

Where this is not feasible, segregation could be done by requiring that the funds be deposited with commercial banks, although this bears the risk of the commercial banks' failure, in which case the reserves could be lost. To mitigate this risk, some countries extend deposit-insurer protection to EMI customers. However, challenges remain for the implementation of such protection, including that it would not cover the risk of misappropriation or fraud by the EMI since the EMI would not be a direct member of the deposit insurer. Other jurisdictions require that the EMI become a direct member of the deposit insurer—thus covering losses due to fraud or misappropriation. But this might clash with the purpose of deposit insurance and impose costs that are not compatible with EMI business models or pose operational challenges that may render them ineffective.

Reaping the benefits from fintech in a sustainable and durable way will require adapting and strengthening financial policy frameworks. Policy makers must put in place a timely and proportionate regulatory and supervisory approach to managing financial risks arising from fintech. Ensuring financial stability, safety, and integrity will remain the core mandates, and these can, in turn, contribute to sustainable development amid healthy innovation and increased competition.

Assessing the fintech landscape and related risks is a prerequisite to identifying regulatory gaps at an early stage. Then authorities can set clear policy goals with a priority on surveillance and oversight mandates. As operational risks are amplified, defining a clear strategy for promoting operational resilience is important. Fintech-related changes may also require financial supervisors to scale up capacity and resources to meet the specific challenges posed by fintech, including through use of regtech and suptech solutions. In addition, domestic and international cooperation is essential to successfully manage cross-sectoral risks, while achieving the benefits of fintech. Finally, if an e-money institution fails, authorities should be well prepared by establishing safe mechanisms to protect customers' funds and to wind down systemic fintechs.

Financial Consumer Protection and Fintech: An Overview of New Manifestations of Consumer Risks and Emerging Regulatory Approaches (Consumer Protection Note) by Gian Boeddu and Jennifer Chien

Fintech is increasingly recognized as a key enabler worldwide for more efficient and competitive financial markets and for expanding access to finance for traditionally underserved consumers.[5] As noted in the Bali Fintech Agenda, launched in October 2018 by the International Monetary Fund (IMF) and the World Bank, fintech can support economic growth and poverty reduction by strengthening financial development, inclusion, and efficiency (IMF and World Bank 2018). The critical challenge for policy makers is to harness the benefits and opportunities of fintech while managing its inherent risks.

New Consumer Risks and New Manifestations of Existing Risks

Some of these risks are new. But many represent new manifestations of existing risks due to the technology that supports and enables fintech offerings—risks from new or changed business models, product features, and provider types, as well as from greater consumer accessibility to sometimes unfamiliar or more complex financial products.[6] For example, a rapid expansion of the peer-to-peer lending (P2PL) market in China in the first half of the 2010s was followed by significant platform collapses, incidents of fraud, and platform operator misconduct, which caused significant losses to consumers.[7] Although digital microcredit has expanded access to credit in some developing economies, countries such as Kenya and Tanzania have seen large numbers of borrowers unable to repay loans owing to irresponsible lending practices.[8]

Similarly, despite significant uptake of electronic money (e-money) in many developing markets, this has been accompanied by a rise in a variety of risks for consumers, including potential loss of funds due to fraud and unscrupulous fee charging. Such negative experiences, in addition to harming consumers directly, may also lead to greater mistrust of fintech and the financial sector overall.

The COVID-19 pandemic has further accelerated the widespread transition of consumers to digital financial services and fintech, highlighting their significant benefits while also demonstrating how risks to consumers can increase in times of crisis and economic stress. For example, reports from Indonesia indicate that individual lenders or investors have been adversely affected by risky loans made through P2PL platforms, as have been borrowers who obtained such loans and are now struggling to get lenders or investors to restructure them.[9] Significant numbers of low-income consumers have faced difficulty repaying existing debts because of the pandemic.[10] Small enterprises have been severely affected by widespread closures and safety measures to slow the spread of COVID-19, thus decreasing enterprises' profitability and impeding repayment obligations.[11] This in turn exposes their investors to increased risk of loss from their investments. In addition, significant increases in fraudulent app-based digital microcredit lenders have been observed during COVID-19 lockdowns (Fu and Mishra 2020).

Authorities responsible for financial consumer protection (FCP) regulations are increasingly faced with the challenge of developing or adapting regulations to address fintech-generated risks to consumers. The task of regulators in developing countries is even more difficult if they tackle this new challenge while having to implement a baseline FCP regulatory framework.[12] In a recent survey, regulators identified their limited internal technical expertise as the foremost impediment to regulating and supervising "alternative finance" (such as P2PL and equity crowdfunding) effectively (World Bank and CCAF 2019, 63).

Objectives of the Note

This note provides (a) an overview of new manifestations of consumer risks that are significant and cross-cutting across four key fintech products: digital microcredit, P2PL, investment-based crowdfunding, and e-money;[13] and (b) examples of emerging regulatory approaches to target such risks. It is based on a more detailed recent World Bank Policy Research Paper, "Consumer Risks in Fintech: New Manifestations of Consumer Risks and Emerging Regulatory Approaches" (World Bank 2021). The research paper delves more deeply into each of the four key fintech products and their associated risks. Its appendix provides an overview of product-specific risks, which the research paper discusses in greater detail.

The primary focus and objective of this note, and the paper on which it is based, is to inform authorities' development of regulatory policy. The examples included here are intended to assist regulators considering potential FCP regulatory approaches to fintech. However, it is hoped that the discussion of manifestations of consumer risks in a fintech context can also assist authorities with related key areas, such as market conduct supervision.

Consumer Risks and Emerging Regulatory Approaches

The key consumer risks and corresponding regulatory approaches discussed in this note are summarized below.

Heightened risks of fraud or misconduct. Several fintech-related factors— such as the novelty and opaqueness of fintech business models, fintech entities' responsibilities in the context of those business models, and a lack of consumer understanding of the new offerings—can heighten the risks of fraud or misconduct by fintech entities or third parties. Platform finance (P2PL and investment-based crowdfunding) poses risks to consumers—lenders or investors as well as borrowers.

Lenders or investors may face losses because of the conduct of platform operators or related parties. These practices may include fraudulent lending or investment opportunities, misappropriation of funds, or facilitation of imprudent lending or investment to generate fee revenue for the operator to the detriment of consumers who ultimately bear the resulting losses. Consumers borrowing from such platforms may similarly suffer harm from the resulting imprudent lending. Holders of e-money also face risks related to agent misconduct, including charging of unauthorized fees, splitting transactions to earn more commissions, and "skimming" into agent accounts. Regulatory approaches to addressing such risks include

- Vetting of fintech entities during the authorization stage;

- Imposing risk management and governance obligations for platform operators;

- Imposing clear responsibility and liability on providers for the conduct of persons acting on their behalf;

- Placing targeted obligations on platform operators to safeguard consumers' interests regardless of business model (such as requiring P2PL platform operators to undertake creditworthiness assessments even if they are not themselves the lender);

- Providing warnings and other key disclosures to consumers regarding the risks associated with fintech products; and

- Segregating client funds.

Conflicts of interest. Certain characteristics of fintech business models can lead to conflicts of interests between consumers and fintech entities. For example, business models heavily dependent on fees generated by new lending business can give rise to perverse incentives for fintech entities to act in a manner inconsistent with the interests of their consumers, such as when P2PL platforms or digital microcredit providers focus on loan quantity over quality to maximize fee-related returns. Such risks can be exacerbated in markets where fintech entities are attempting to grow their revenues and size quickly.

Potentially harmful conflicts can also arise where fintech entities are empowered to make decisions affecting the risk of loss on loans but where consumers bear that risk—such as when a P2PL or crowdfunding platform operator assists with loan or investment selections without performing adequate due diligence.

Corresponding regulatory approaches include placing positive obligations on fintech entities to

- Manage and mitigate conflicts of interest;

- Act in accordance with the best interests of their consumers;

- Undertake adequate assessments regardless of business model; and

- Prohibit business arrangements that encourage conflicted behavior.

Platform unreliability or vulnerability to cyber threats. Consumers may face a heightened risk of adverse impacts from platform or technology unreliability or vulnerability. They may be more vulnerable to cyber fraud when acquiring fintech products than when accessing financial products through more traditional channels, because interaction with fintech providers is largely or exclusively via digital and remote means. Platform or other technology malfunctions can negatively affect consumers in ways ranging from inconvenience and poor service to monetary loss and loss of data integrity—the risk of which may increase because of heavier reliance on automated transaction processing.

Regulatory approaches to addressing such risks include specific obligations on fintech entities to address technology and systems-related risks and risks associated with outsourcing.

Fintech business failures. Some fintech entities may be at greater risk of business failure or insolvency than established financial service providers because of inexperience, untested businesses, and market factors affecting long-term viability. This can mean that consumers whose funds are held or administered by a fintech entity face correspondingly greater risk of loss if the provider becomes insolvent or the business ceases to operate. Consumers may risk losing their committed loan principals and investment funds or repayments as well as earned investment returns being held or administered by a P2PL or crowdfunding platform that fails. Insolvency of e-money issuers or banks holding e-money floats similarly puts client funds at risk, especially where there is no deposit insurance.

Regulatory approaches to address such risks include requirements for fintech entities to segregate their clients' funds from other funds and to have in place business-continuity and resolution arrangements.

Disclosure and transparency issues. The digital environment poses inherent challenges for disclosure and transparency, amplified by the novelty of fintech product offerings and consumers' lack of experience with such products. Information provided via digital channels may not be appropriately formatted for consumer understanding or retention. Poor design of user interfaces may hamper consumer comprehension or exploit behavioral biases by concealing or underplaying "negative" aspects such as risks and costs. Fintech can also give consumers access to products, such as P2PL or crowdfunding investment opportunities, to which they may have had limited or no previous exposure, thus making clear and understandable information even more essential for good decision-making.

Approaches to address such issues include requirements to disclose key information in a consistent and clear format, on a timely basis, and in a manner that can be retained by consumers. Behavioral insights can also be used to disclose information via digital channels in a manner that aims to increase the likelihood of consumer comprehension.

Consumer inexperience. Consumers' inexperience or lack of sophistication can potentially heighten the risks when they acquire fintech products. With fintech development consumers increasingly have access to novel and complex financial products, but they may lack the knowledge or experience to assess or use these products properly. For example, platform finance enables more individuals to act as investors and lenders. This has positive implications for financial inclusion but can enhance the risks to ordinary consumers who are new to assessing these more complex opportunities.

Potential regulatory approaches include

- Limiting individual investments, such as through overall caps on how much an individual may borrow through a P2PL platform or how much money a company can raise on a crowdfunding platform;

- Imposing limitations on specific types of investors or exposures;

- Providing targeted warnings to potential investors;

- Requiring consumers to confirm that they understand the risks they are undertaking; and

- Requiring cooling-off periods.

Risks may also arise regarding digital microcredit products being offered to consumers that are unsuitable and unaffordable. Regulatory approaches include requiring effective creditworthiness assessments and applying product design and governance principles, particularly where automated credit scoring is used.

Algorithm-related risks. Use of algorithms for consumer-related decisions is becoming particularly prevalent in highly automated fintech business models. Consumers may face a range of risks as a result, such as discriminatory or biased outcomes.

Emerging regulatory approaches in this context include

- Applying fair treatment and antidiscrimination obligations to algorithmic processes;

- Establishing governance frameworks that require procedures, controls, and safeguards on the development, testing, and deployment of algorithms to ensure fairness;

- Imposing auditing requirements; and

- Establishing consumer rights regarding how they or their information may be subjected to algorithmic decision-making.

Additional Considerations

It is not the intent of this note to suggest that all risk mitigants it discusses should be implemented. For any regulator contemplating implementing the kinds of regulatory measures discussed in this note, it will be important to prioritize and take a risk-based approach, to tailor regulatory approaches to country context, and to balance the need for consumer protection with the resulting impact on industry and market development and innovation. Moreover, it would not necessarily be advisable for a country to implement all of the regulatory measures discussed in this note immediately or to transplant approaches from other jurisdictions without adjustment. This note also summarizes a range of key implementation matters for regulators to consider.

Specific Fintech Products

Innovation in Payments: Opportunities and Challenges for EMDEs (Payments Note) by Dorothee Delort and Jose Antonio Garcia Luna

The global economy is undergoing a rapid digital transformation that is changing many conventional notions about our behavior and preferences. This includes the way in which we—as consumers, as businesses, or in interactions with government—seek out goods and services and pay for them or how we receive money from others or transfer it to family or friends. As the payments industry undergoes radical changes from digital transformation, users, providers of payment services, and regulators are adapting to the new dynamics at varying paces.

This note discusses the most significant innovations in payments and their key impacts and implications on users, banks and other payment service providers, regulators, and the overall structure of the payments market. The note places special emphasis on how emerging markets and developing economies (EMDEs) can reap the benefits of payment innovations in terms of costs, convenience, accessibility, and inclusion for individuals and firms while leapfrogging development of their payments markets and effectively supporting economic activity.

Payments are probably the financial activity most affected by innovation, undergoing radical changes from various perspectives. This transformation has been prompted by the adoption of new technologies and business models, by the emergence of new market players, and by changes in the structure of the market. This is having a profound impact beyond the realm of payments and is also affecting the real economy. The following changes are significant:

- *Payments have become a stand-alone product,* no longer just a supporting function typically offered only by banks as part of a bundle of services and with comfortable profit margins. In other words, payments have become a separate, identifiable service offered by a growing number of providers, including nonbanks, exercising downward pressure on fees and margins and fueling upward demand for quality.

- *The consumer experience has been transformed* as long-standing barriers or deterrents to the use of digital payments are gradually being overcome, helping meet new demands from payers and payees for increased speed and convenience and lower prices.

- *The purchase experience has been totally transformed*—in cases such as ride-hailing or meal-ordering apps or "one-click" online ordering—by making the actual payment process "invisible" from the customer's perspective.

- *Payments are increasingly becoming a source and provider of data* that are critical for differentiation against competitors and for the provision of other products and services, including—but not limited to—those offered by financial sector entities.

- *Innovation in payments has enabled and shaped major developments in the real economy,* like the surge of e-commerce—including transactional online services offered by governments—and, in turn, new platform models that have placed additional demands on payment services.

Competition in payments has increased and is only intensifying, but may paradoxically lead to renewed concentration and an oligopolistic equilibrium. In essence, payments may evolve once again into a concentrated market served by a relatively limited number of providers. Unlike in the past, these providers could be technology giants or large telecommunication firms rather than banking institutions. The consequences and challenges of this potential outcome are not fully understood.

Although innovation in retail payments has been prolific, it has not been fully transmitted to specific payment streams like international remittances and other forms of cross-border payments, some types of government payments, and business-to-business (B2B) payments.[14] For example, the Committee on Payments and Market Infrastructures reports that cross-border payments lag behind domestic payments in terms of cost, speed, access, and transparency (CPMI 2020).

In the area of government payments, many EMDEs have a long way to go in digitizing their payments and collections effectively, largely because of coordination challenges and other elements that slow down the general use of payment innovations. Here, however, the COVID-19 crisis has accelerated digitization efforts—for example to facilitate transfer of relief funds while trying to ensure social distancing.

As for B2B payments, this market segment has certain unique requirements like linkage to invoicing processes and taxation, and payments tend to be for larger amounts. To date, these unique requirements have not been fully met.

Innovations in payments and their consequences on service providers and the overall payments market are also proving to be a unique challenge for central banks in their various statutory roles regarding payments (box B.1).[15] The regulatory and oversight roles of central banks are already being challenged by the innovation-driven changes in the structure of the payments market. Furthermore, innovations may even disrupt the traditional divide between central bank money and commercial bank money, thus affecting all aspects of the central bank's mission beyond its mandate on payments, including monetary policy and financial stability. Central banks have no choice but to introduce changes in their own work processes and procedures, build new capacities, and, more generally, rethink their approach to money. Their role is not diminished by innovation in payments; it is, on the contrary, made even more critical.

EMDEs can greatly benefit from many of these innovations but will need to carefully consider their multiple facets and implications and develop policies

---

BOX B.1

Characterizing Innovations in Payments

Innovation in payments can be characterized on three levels: how it materializes, its structural impact, and how the central bank, as payments authority, needs to adapt. The main pillars of innovation in payments include (a) changes to the way payment services are linked to an account; (b) changes to the systems that process payment transactions; and (c) changes in the way consumers interact with payments and the business model of payment service providers.

Thanks to innovations like mobile wallets or super apps—combined with fast payments, application programming interfaces (APIs), and other technologies—customers now find it more convenient and less costly to make and receive digital payments while also enjoying a smoother user experience. At the same time, innovations are redefining business models for payments, which in turn is having far-reaching consequences for the very structure of the payments market.

The most conspicuous effects of innovation on the structure of the market have been its impact on competition by opening up the payments market to nonbanks, by putting downward pressure on payment service fees, and by making real-time payments the new normal. While new entrants challenge incumbents, innovation could end up having a paradoxical, centralizing effect and a tendency to increase concentration, with the major transformation being the shift of dominant market positions from incumbents to Big Tech firms. In addition to banks, other payments ecosystem players are deeply affected by the ongoing changes, especially so for international and domestic payment card networks and Automated Clearing House (ACH) service providers. Government agencies are also significantly affected by the wave of innovation in payments—particularly in their interactions with citizens through the provision of government services and programs that involve making payments.

Innovation in payments challenges central banks in their typical roles in relation to payments—that is, as operators, overseers, regulators, and catalysts for change. They must also move beyond their typical mandates on payments as innovations continue to redefine money. The combination of traditional and new risks and causes for potential market failures calls for central banks to reassess and renew, not just policies, but also their internal organization, activities, and tools, while also heightening their collaboration and cooperation with authorities and stakeholders.

and institutional capacities accordingly. EMDEs should continue to create an enabling environment for innovation in their financial sector, fostering new products and providers while managing risks and protecting consumers. At the same time, they should not write off proven strategies and methods to accomplish important objectives like financial inclusion and stability. In any case, central banks and other regulators should be duly equipped and prepared to support their country's public and private sector actors so that they can maximize gains from the new reality.

Fintech and SME Finance: Expanding Responsible Access (SME note) by Ghada Teima, Ivor Istuk, Luis Maldonado, Miguel Soriano, and John Wilson

Small and medium enterprises (SMEs) represent the economic backbone of most developed and emerging countries. Globally, they account for more than 90 percent of all businesses and more than 50 percent of employment.[16] SMEs are also significant contributors of economic activity, representing on average 60–70 percent of the GDP of most countries worldwide.

Although SMEs play a major role in the economy, their lack of access to finance often poses a critical barrier for them. SMEs cannot obtain adequate access to finance for many reasons, including the higher cost to reach and serve SMEs relative to the financial service revenue potential; information asymmetries that affect the availability of financial and credit data needed to assess their creditworthiness; lack of collateral; lack of financial literacy; and difficulties in registration and verification.

Digital financial services (DFS) can help close the financing gap for SMEs by providing access to alternative sources of funding and improving access to traditional players by enabling new digital products and process automation. Digitization and automation make the financing process more efficient, thereby lowering costs. The use of alternative data sources and Big Data analytics provides additional information sources to the credit risk-assessment process, allowing SMEs that were once unable to obtain finance to gain access. New business models, such as the sharing economy, e-commerce, digitization of SME-business processes, and open banking and application programming interfaces (APIs), provide rich data on SMEs' activities and cash flows. These developments enable DFS and help SMEs obtain access to financial products.

Globally, millions of small businesses are at risk of closing permanently or have suffered massive losses because of the COVID-19 pandemic. In a crisis, SMEs are more vulnerable than large corporations in terms of access to finance. Speed of execution is critical for providing government relief funds to SMEs, and digital financial products have been essential to supporting SMEs during the pandemic.

However, certain obstacles and challenges still make it difficult for SMEs to fully adopt digital financial products. These are the main areas where challenges have been identified: digital financial literacy and awareness of DFS, digital infrastructure, financial supervision and regulation, identity, and data privacy and data protection. Some of the issues are more prevalent in emerging markets, which tend to have less developed digital infrastructure, systems, and processes.

Recommendations

Policy and regulatory approaches can facilitate access to finance for SMEs through DFS. Foundational elements where policy can have a positive impact include

- Digital financial education programs for SMEs highlighting DFS awareness;

- Affordable digital infrastructure that fosters widespread internet access and usage, along with robust cybersecurity frameworks;

- Financial regulatory frameworks that encourage financial innovation while minimizing the risks created by digital financial products;

- Robust, secure, and universally accepted company ID and registration frameworks for SMEs; and

- Adequate data protection and data privacy regulations.

In addition, policy and regulatory recommendations that are specific to digital financial products for SME financing can be classified around the following themes:

- Promote the digitization of SMEs' operations, improve the availability of SME information, expand credit information sharing, and support efficient and widely accessible digital payment systems

- Develop modern credit infrastructure frameworks to support the introduction of fintech asset-based lending products for SMEs

- Support the growth and development of debt and equity capital platforms to improve SME access to finance through the establishment of regulatory frameworks that balance innovation with investor and consumer protection.

What Does Digital Money Mean for Emerging Market and Developing Economies? (Digital Money Note) by Erik Feyen, Jon Frost, Harish Natarajan, and Tara Rice

Physical cash and commercial bank money are dominant vehicles for retail payments around the world, including in emerging markets and developing economies (EMDEs). Yet payments in EMDEs are marked by several key deficiencies—such as lack of universal access to transaction accounts, widespread informality, limited competition, and high costs, particularly for cross-border payments. Digital money seeks to address these deficiencies.

This note categorizes new digital money proposals. These include crypto-assets, stablecoins, and central bank digital currencies (CBDCs). It assesses the supply and demand factors that may determine which countries are more likely to adopt these innovations. It also lays out particular policy challenges for authorities in EMDEs. Finally, it compares these digital money proposals with digital innovations such as mobile money, retail fast-payment systems, new products by incumbent financial institutions, and new entrants such as specialized cross-border money transfer operators.

Proposals for global stablecoins have put a much-needed spotlight on deficiencies in financial inclusion and in cross-border payments and remittances in EMDEs. Yet stablecoin initiatives are no panacea. Although they may achieve adoption in certain EMDEs, they may also pose particular development, macroeconomic, and cross-border challenges for these countries and have not been tested at scale. Several EMDE authorities are weighing the potential costs and benefits of CBDCs. The authors argue that the distinction between token-based and account-based money matters less than the distinction between central bank and non-central bank money. Fast-moving fintech innovations that are built on or improve existing financial plumbing may address many of the issues in EMDEs that both private stablecoins and CBDCs aim to tackle.

Notes

1. Nascent but rapidly evolving digital financial products and services such as central bank digital currencies, crypto-assets, stablecoins, and decentralized finance are beyond the scope of the current version of this index.

2. "Insurance companies" has been used as a generic term for insurers of all types.

3. Unless specified otherwise, the term "respondent" refers to the institutions that chose to respond to the specific question or questions being discussed.

4. Big Tech firms are large companies with established technology platforms, such as Alibaba, Amazon, Apple, Baidu, eBay, Facebook, Google, and Microsoft. Big Techs that offer financial services are a subset of fintech firms—a broader class of technology firms (many of which are smaller than Big Tech firms) that offer financial services (BIS 2019).

5. For the purposes of this note, "fintech" refers to advances in technology that have the potential to transform the provision of financial services, spurring the development of new business models, applications, processes, and products (IMF and World Bank 2018, 12).

6. For an overview of risks and benefits in a digital financial services context, see OECD (2020, 12–14).

7. See, for example, CAFI (2018, 42); Owens (2018, 8–9); Hornby and Zhang (2018); and Huang (2018, 77).

8. For example, a 2017 MicroSave study found that 2.7 million Kenyans were blacklisted in credit reference bureaus in the past three years, 400,000 of these for amounts of less than US$2 (Mustafa et al. 2017).

9. See, for example, Faridi (2020).

10. For example, 80 percent, 87 percent, and 90 percent of low-income survey respondents in Ghana, India, and Kenya, respectively, indicated they were late in making loan repayments since the pandemic began (as of April 11–12, 2020) (Amin 2020).

11. See, for example, Gibbens (2020).

12. For an overview of key elements of an FCP regulatory framework (being an element of a broader legal and supervisory framework for FCP), see, for example, World Bank (2017, 14, 68, 102, 140).

13. These products were selected as examples of fintech offerings that may address some of the most basic needs of first-time, and thus inexperienced, financial consumers—namely, making payments, borrowing, saving, or investing money—as well as representing different stages in the development of fintech product offerings and corresponding regulatory and policy frameworks that surround them.

14. In addition, some relevant developments in large-value payments have been less visible for nonpayments specialists and the general population. These include the adoption of the International Organization for Standardization (ISO) multipart ISO 20022 message standards, cloud-based hosting of payment solutions, and expanding access to large-value payment systems to participants other than banks.

15. These roles include being operators of payment systems; supervisors of payment services providers; catalysts for change; and overseers of national payments systems, which encompass payment systems, payment services, and payment instruments.

16. SME business, employment, and GDP data from "Small and Medium Enterprises (SMEs) Finance," topic page, World Bank website: https://www.worldbank.org/en/topic/smefinance.

References

Appaya, Sharmista, Matei Dohotaru, Byungnam Ahn, Tatsiana Kliatskova, Prasanna Seshan, and Ion Pascaru. 2020. "A Roadmap to SupTech Solutions for Low Income (IDA) Countries." Fintech Note No. 7, World Bank, Washington, DC.

Amin, Ashirul. 2020. "The Impact of COVID-19 on Financial Lives in Eight Countries, over Two Weeks." Dipstick Survey report, BFA Global, Nairobi and Boston.

BIS (Bank for International Settlements). 2019. "Big Tech in Finance: Opportunities and Risks." In *Annual Economic Report 2019*, 55–79. Basel, Switzerland: BIS.

Boeddu, Gian, and Jennifer Chien. 2022. "Financial Consumer Protection and Fintech: An Overview of New Manifestations of Consumer Risks and Emerging Regulatory Approaches." Consumer Protection Note for *Fintech and the Future of Finance*, World Bank, Washington, DC.

CAFI (Chinese Academy of Financial Inclusion). 2018. "Growing with Pain: Digital Financial Inclusion in China." Report, CAFI at Renmin University of China, Beijing.

CPMI (Committee on Payments and Market Infrastructures). 2020. *Enhancing Cross-Border Payments: Building Blocks of a Global Roadmap*. Basel: Bank for International Settlements.

Delort, Dorothee, and Jose Antonio Garcia Luna. 2022. "Innovation in Payments: Opportunities and Challenges for EMDEs." Payments Note for *Fintech and the Future of Finance*, World Bank Group, Washington, DC.

Didier, Tatiana, Erik Feyen, Ruth Llovet Montanes, and Oya Ardic. 2022. "Global Patterns of Fintech Activity and Enabling Factors." Fintech Activity Note for *Fintech and the Future of Finance*, World Bank, Washington, DC.

Faridi, Omar. 2020. "P2P Fintech Lending Sector in Indonesia May Struggle Due to Risky Loans as Lenders Rejected over 50% of Restructuring Requests." Crowdfund Insider, June 11.

Feyen, Erik, Jon Frost, Leonardo Gambacorta, Harish Natarajan, and Matthew Saal. 2022a. "Fintech and the Digital Transformation of Financial Services: Implications for Market Structure and Public Policy." Market Structure Note for *Fintech and the Future of Finance*, World Bank, Washington, DC.

Feyen, Erik, Jon Frost, Harish Natarajan, and Tara Rice. 2022b. "What Does Digital Money Mean for Emerging Market and Developing Economies?" Digital Money Note for *Fintech and the Future of Finance*, World Bank, Washington, DC.

Feyen, Erik, Harish Natarajan, Guillermo Galicia Rabadan, Robert Paul Heffernan, Matthew Saal, and Arpita Sarkar. 2022c. "World Bank Group Global Market Survey: Digital Technology and the Future of Finance." Fintech Market Participants Survey for *Fintech and the Future of Finance*, World Bank, Washington, DC.

Fu, Jonathan, and Mrinal Mishra. 2020. "Combating the Rise in Fraudulent Fintech Apps." *CFI Blog*, December 21, 2020.

Gibbens, Elizabeth. 2020. "Helping Small Businesses Navigate through COVID-19." *IFC Insights* Issue No. 6 (March 31), International Finance Corporation, Washington, DC.

Gispert, Tatiana Alonso, Pierre-Laurent Chatain, Karl Driessen, Danilo Palermo, and Ariadne Plaitakis. 2022. "Regulation and Supervision of Fintech: Considerations for EMDE Policymakers." Regulation Note for *Fintech and the Future of Finance*, World Bank, Washington, DC.

Hornby, Lucy, and Archie Zhang. 2018. "China's Middle Class Hit by Shadow Banking Defaults." *Financial Times*, December 26.

Huang, (Robin) Hui. 2018. "Online P2P Lending and Regulatory Responses in China: Opportunities and Challenges." *European Business Organization Law Review* 19 (1): 63–92.

IMF (International Monetary Fund) and World Bank. 2018. "The Bali Fintech Agenda." Chapeau paper, September 19, IMF and World Bank, Washington, DC.

Mustafa, Zeituna, Mercy Wachira, Vera Bersudskaya, William Nanjero, and Graham A. N. Wright. 2017. "Where Credit Is Due: Customer Experience of Digital Credit in Kenya." PowerPoint presentation, March 2017, MicroSave Consulting, Lucknow, India.

OECD (Organisation for Economic Co-operation and Development). 2020. "Financial Consumer Protection Policy Approaches in the Digital Age: Protecting Consumers' Assets, Data and Privacy." Policy guidance note developed under the work program of the G20/OECD Task Force on Financial Consumer Protection, OECD, Paris.

Owens, John. 2018. "Responsible Digital Credit: What Does Responsible Digital Credit Look Like?" Report, Center for Financial Inclusion at Accion, Washington, DC.

Teima, Ghada, Ivor Istuk, Luis Maldonado, Miguel Soriano, and John Wilson. 2022. "Fintech and SME Finance: Expanding Responsible Access." SME Note for *Fintech and the Future of Finance*, World Bank, Washington, DC.

World Bank. 2017. "Good Practices for Financial Consumer Protection, 2017 Edition." Report, World Bank, Washington, DC.

World Bank. 2021. "Consumer Risks in Fintech: New Manifestations of Consumer Risks and Emerging Regulatory Approaches." Policy Research Paper, World Bank, Washington, DC.

World Bank and CCAF (Cambridge Centre for Alternative Finance). 2019. "Regulating Alternative Finance: Results from a Global Regulator Survey." Report, World Bank, Washington, DC; CCAF, Judge Business School, University of Cambridge.

Acceleration of Fintech Use during the COVID-19 Pandemic

Globally, the pandemic has intensified fintech use. Social distancing and other containment measures adopted on a global scale to mitigate the spread of COVID-19 have increased the benefits of digital financial services (DFS). Traditional financial services are predominantly built on cash transactions and face-to-face interactions with financial service providers—interactions that were eliminated in favor of social distancing. DFS, on the other hand, could proceed because they are largely predicated on remote, contactless, and cashless payments and transactions.

In several emerging markets and developing economies, mobile money activity declined as the pandemic struck, alongside the overall decline in economic activity. As lockdowns were lifted, mobile money transactions recovered and grew to levels well above the prepandemic baseline, even allowing for trend growth. Registered accounts grew by 13 percent with active accounts growing by 17 percent, indicating that many users who had registered but not used their accounts were now active (GSMA 2021). Transaction volume rose by 15 percent and the value of transactions by 22 percent. One study found that, in the United States, fintech use during the pandemic rose from 36 percent to 42 percent among consumers surveyed (Krivkovich et al. 2020).

The pandemic also accelerated providers' plans for digital transformation. More than 80 percent of all Fintech Market Participants Survey respondents felt that COVID-19 had increased the need for fintech and digital transformation (Feyen et al. 2022). Digitization in customer channels, product adaptation, and internal processes were strategic priorities.

Consumer behavior also changed because of the pandemic. The Fintech Activity Note looked at novel app download data (Didier et al. 2022). This data set, reflecting the stream of new users of financial apps, provided insights into DFS adoption worldwide during the COVID-19 pandemic.

The analysis in the Fintech Activity Note showed a marked spike in worldwide financial app downloads, especially of nonbank financial apps, during the first peak months of the pandemic. The increase is particularly marked for nonbank financial apps. Global downloads of nonbank financial apps increased by 45 percent, from an average of about 7 million downloads per day during the last quarter of 2019 to a peak of over 10 million on April 15, 2020—around the same time as the peak of policy measures taken to constrain community mobility (Didier et al. 2022).

The analysis also shows a robust positive correlation at the country level between the growth in downloads of the top 100 financial apps since the outbreak of the pandemic and the severity of the impact of COVID-19, even after controlling for gross domestic product per capita and demographic characteristics (figure C.1). Moreover, the estimations indicate that the increase in financial app downloads was related to the stringency of community mobility policies or practices rather than the contagion of the disease itself in a given country.

FIGURE C.1 Worldwide Downloads of Financial Apps before and during the COVID-19 Pandemic

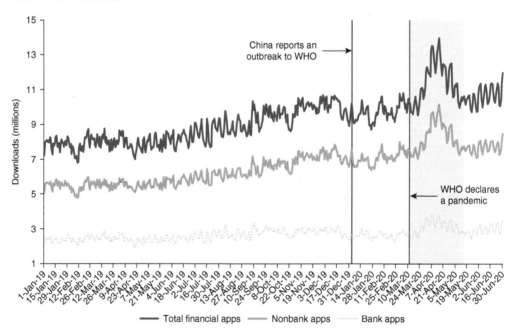

Source: Didier et al. 2022.
Note: The figure shows worldwide downloads of the top 100 financial apps for each country in the sample, after controlling for GDP per capita and demographic characteristics. The sample included 125 countries across all regions and income levels. WHO = World Health Organization.

References

Didier, Tatiana, Erik Feyen, Ruth Llovet Montañés, and Oya Ardic. 2022. "Global Patterns of Fintech Activity and Enabling Factors." Fintech Activity Note for *Fintech and the Future of Finance*, World Bank, Washington, DC.

Feyen, Erik, Harish Natarajan, Guillermo Galicia Rabadan, Robert Paul Heffernan, Matthew Saal, and Arpita Sarkar. 2022. "World Bank Group Global Market Survey: Digital Technology and the Future of Finance." Fintech Market Participants Survey for *Fintech and the Future of Finance*, World Bank, Washington, DC.

GSMA (Global System for Mobile Communications Association). 2021. "State of the Industry Report on Mobile Money 2021." GSMA, London.

Krivkovich, Alexis, Olivia White, Zac Townsend, and John Euart. 2020. "How US Customers' Attitudes to Fintech Are Shifting during the Pandemic." Our Insights, McKinsey & Company, December 17.

APPENDIX D

Open Banking Frameworks in Selected Countries

TABLE D.1 **Open Banking Authorities and Regulatory Approaches, by Country**

Country	Authority driving open banking	Regulatory approach
Australia	Australian Competition and Consumer Commission (ACCC)	Mandatory
Brazil	Central Bank of Brazil	Hybrid (mandatory for larger banks and conglomerates and voluntary for the rest)
Canada	Government of Canada	In development (as of November 2022)
Colombia	Regulatory Projection and Financial Regulation Studies Unit (URF) but Central Bank of Colombia will implement	Voluntary
European Union	European Union	Mandatory
Georgia	National Bank of Georgia	Mandatory
India	Reserve Bank of India (RBI) and National Payments Corporation of India (NPCI)	Mandatory
Indonesia	Bank Indonesia (BI) and Financial Services Authority (OKJ)	Voluntary (API standardization)
Malaysia	Central Bank of Malaysia (BNM)	Voluntary

(Continued)

TABLE D.1 Open Banking Authorities and Regulatory Approaches, by Country *(continued)*

Country	Authority driving open banking	Regulatory approach
Mexico	National Banking and Stock Commission (CNBV) and Bank of Mexico (Banxico)	Mandatory
New Zealand	Industry-led supported by the government	Voluntary
Nigeria	Central Bank of Nigeria	Voluntary
Singapore	Monetary Authority of Singapore (MAS)	Voluntary
The Philippines	Central Bank of the Philippines (BSP)	To be determined
Türkiye	Banking Regulation and Supervision Agency (BRSA)	Mandatory
United Kingdom	Competition and Markets Authority (CMA)	Mandatory
United States	Consumer Financial Protection Bureau (CFPB)	Voluntary

Source: World Bank.
Note: Shaded rows designate advanced economies (as classified by the International Monetary Fund's *World Economic Outlook*). API = application programming interface.

Principles for Ethical Use of Artificial Intelligence and Data Analytics

Various bodies are developing principles to ensure the ethical use of artificial intelligence (AI) and data analytics. Two such examples are described below.

European Commission

The European Commission (EC) issued guidelines on the ethical use of AI in 2019 (since updated in 2021) as government authorities and private companies explore the opportunities and risks of this new technology. The guidelines list seven key principles for ethical development of AI, including ensuring human agency and oversight, privacy and data governance, nondiscriminatory and non-biased algorithms, accountability in the systems, and robustness and traceability of AI systems (AI HLEG 2019).

The principles state that besides ensuring full respect for privacy and data protection, adequate data governance mechanisms must also be ensured, considering the quality and integrity of the data and ensuring legitimized access to data. It must be ensured that data collected about individuals will not be used to unlawfully or unfairly discriminate against them. The principles also require that AI systems be protected against vulnerabilities that may lead to data poisoning and may influence the data or the system's behavior. In addition, the guidelines state that, considering the principle of proportionality between means and ends, AI developers should always prefer public sector data to personal data.

Monetary Authority of Singapore

The Monetary Authority of Singapore's fairness, ethics, accountability, and transparency (FEAT) principles to promote responsible use of AI and data analytics is another useful framework to govern the use of data. Some of the key principles include fairness, accountability (both internal and external), and transparency—specifically, (a) that data-driven models be regularly evaluated and validated to minimize data-driven biases, and (b) that people be informed of the data being used to make decisions and how the data affect them, taking into account verified relevant supplementary data provided by data subjects (MAS 2018).

References

AI HLEG (High-Level Expert Group on Artificial Intelligence). 2019. "Ethics Guidelines for Trustworthy AI." Guidelines document produced by the Independent AI HLEG set up by the European Commission, Brussels.

MAS (Monetary Authority of Singapore). 2018. "Principles to Promote Fairness, Ethics, Accountability and Transparency (FEAT) in the Use of Artificial Intelligence and Data Analytics in Singapore's Financial Sector." Statement of principles, MAS, Singapore.

Glossary

account-based payment instruments	Payment instruments that access funds held in accounts in contrast to some digital asset-based payment instruments where the funds are held in a decentralized manner without need for any account-holding institution. Account-based payment instruments can include account-based central bank digital currencies (CBDCs) and those linked to accounts held at banks and other deposit-taking institutions, and prepaid accounts—e-money and mobile money.
advanced economies (AEs)	Countries classified as "advanced economies" by the International Monetary Fund's *World Economic Outlook* (IMF 2020)
Aggregate Fintech Activity Index	Indicator of fintech activity across countries developed in the Fintech Activity Note (Didier et al. 2022), measured from 2014 to 2018, taking into consideration four activities: (a) equity investments in fintech companies, (b) use of fintech credit (facilitated by electronic or online platforms), (c) use of digital payment services by households and firms, and (d) downloads of finance smartphone apps

algorithmic decision-making	The use of data inputs and statistical models to make decisions—for example, to approve a payment instruction or approve a loan. Such algorithms often analyze large amounts of data (for example, Big Data—*see below*) to infer correlations or, more generally, to derive information deemed useful to make decisions. Humans may be "in the loop" to varying degrees, depending on how the decision is calculated, reviewed, and implemented in a given business process.
AML/CFT measures: anti-money laundering and combating (or countering) the financing of terrorism	Laws, regulations, and supervisory and enforcement actions to prevent, detect, investigate, or prosecute movements or deposits of funds that proceed from or fund crime See also Financial Action Task Force (FATF).
anti-tying rules	Legal provisions that prohibit a company (such as a bank) from offering a product or service on the condition that a customer either (a) obtain another product or service from the company or one of its affiliates, or (b) refrain from obtaining a tied product from the company's competitors
application programming interface (API)	A set of rules and specifications for software programs to communicate with each other, hence forming an interface between different programs to facilitate their interaction
artificial intelligence (AI)	Theory and development of computer systems able to perform tasks that traditionally have required human intelligence. As a field, AI has existed for many years. However, recent increases in computing power coupled with increases in the availability and quantity of data have resulted in a resurgence of interest in potential AI applications. These applications are already being used to diagnose diseases, translate languages, and drive cars—and they are increasingly being used in the financial sector as well (FSB 2017a).
asset-based lending (ABL)	Lending products that are secured by movable property assets. Such assets may be tangibles (such as plant or equipment and inventory, crops, livestock, and invoices) or intangibles (such as trademarks and patents). ABL products include factoring, reverse factoring, secured revolving lines of credit, merchant cash advances secured by future receipts, and equipment or financial leasing.

Automated Clearing House (ACH)	An electronic clearing system in which payment orders are exchanged between financial institutions, primarily via magnetic media or telecommunications networks, and then cleared among the participants. All operations are handled by a data processing center. An ACH typically clears credit transfers, debit transfers, and in some cases also checks.
Bali Fintech Agenda (BFA)	A set of 12 policy elements developed by the International Monetary Fund (IMF) and the World Bank, aimed at helping member countries to harness the benefits and opportunities of fintech, while managing the inherent risks (IMF 2018)
banking as a service (BaaS)	Business model in which fintech firms and other third parties that meet a bank's security, legal, and compliance requirements integrate banking products into their own offerings without obtaining their own banking licenses, allowing them to leverage the bank's regulatory infrastructure. BaaS business models are often implemented by directly connecting to the bank's systems via application programming interfaces (APIs).
Basel Core Principles (BCPs)	The 29 Core Principles for Effective Banking Supervision (Core Principles) are minimum global standards for the sound prudential regulation and supervision of banks, initially published by the Basel Committee for Banking Supervision in 1997 and updated in 2006 and 2012 (BCBS 2012).
Big Data	A generic term that designates the massive volume of data that is generated by the increasing use of digital tools and information systems
Big Tech	A large company whose primary activity is in digital services and has a large digital services customer base. Examples of Big Techs include online search engines, social media platforms, e-commerce platforms, ride-hailing platforms, and mobile network operators. Numerous Big Techs have started to offer financial services, leveraging their large customer bases and the data they have on transactions and activities that give rise to payments or a need for credit, insurance, or other financial services. Examples include Alibaba, Facebook, Grab, and Safaricom.
blockchain	A form of distributed ledger in which details of transactions are held in the ledger in the form of blocks of information. A block of new information is attached into the chain of preexisting blocks via a computerized process by which transactions are validated (FSB 2019). See also distributed ledger technology.

cash-in, cash-out (CICO) network	A network that enables the conversion of e-money into cash or vice versa. Mobile money agent networks providing such services are sometimes referred to as "CICO networks."
central bank digital currency (CBDC)	CBDC is not a well-defined term and is used to refer to a number of concepts. However, it is envisioned by most to be a new form of central bank money—that is, a central bank liability, denominated in an existing unit of account, that can serve both as a medium of exchange and a store of value. A CBDC is a digital form of central bank money that is different from balances in traditional reserve or settlement accounts (CPMI 2018).
challenger bank	A newly licensed bank competing with established financial institutions. "Challenger banks" emerged as a phrase in the UK market to denote greenfield banks built from scratch and unrelated to the dominant financial service providers in the market. The entry of challenger banks was encouraged to increase competition following the 2008–09 Global Financial Crisis. Metro Bank (the first new bank license issued in the UK in 100 years), Virgin Money, and others focused on improving the retail branch experience. Some challenger banks such as Starling, Oak North, and others rely more exclusively on digital channels.
cloud computing	An innovation in computing that allows for the use of an online network ("cloud") of hosting processors to increase the scale and flexibility of computing capacity (FSB 2019)
contextualized finance	The provision of a financial service in the context, or integrated into the workflow, of another activity (for example, integration of payments into the ride activity on a ride-hailing platform, or taking out a loan on an e-commerce platform) See also embedded finance.
core banking systems	Systems used by commercial banks and other financial institutions to manage the operations of their "core" products like current and saving accounts and loans
correspondent banking	An arrangement under which one bank (correspondent) holds deposits owned by other banks (respondents) and provides those banks with payment and other services (CPMI 2016a)
combating (or countering) financing of terrorism (CFT)	See AML/CFT measures.

credit reporting system	Credit reporting systems comprise the institutions, individuals, rules, procedures, standards, and technology that enable information flows relevant to making decisions related to credit and loan agreements. At their core, credit reporting systems consist of databases of information on debtors, together with the institutional, technological, and legal framework supporting the efficient functioning of such databases. The information stored in these systems can relate to individuals or businesses (World Bank 2011).
credit scoring	A statistical method for evaluating the probability that a prospective borrower will fulfill its financial obligations associated with a loan (World Bank 2011)
cross-border payments	Funds transfers for which the senders' and the recipients' payment service providers are located in different jurisdictions. Cross-border payments may or may not involve a currency conversion (FSB 2020b, 2021).
crowdfunding	The practice of matching people and companies raising funds with those seeking to invest for a financial return without the involvement of traditional financial intermediaries. The matching process is performed by a web-based platform that solicits funds for specific purposes from the public. Depending on the type of funding provided, we distinguish between loan crowdfunding and equity crowdfunding. In either case, individual contracts are established between those in need of funding and those seeking to invest or lend, so that the platform itself does not undertake any risk transformation (Ehrentraud, Ocampo, and Vega 2020).
crypto-assets	A type of private digital asset that depends primarily on cryptography and distributed ledger or similar technology (FSB 2020a)
crypto exchange	A platform that typically provides customers with buying, selling, transfer, and custody services related to crypto-assets. A crypto exchange is an example of a virtual-asset service provider (VASP).
customer due diligence (CDD)	Processes used by financial institutions to collect and evaluate relevant information about a customer or potential customer
cyber risk	The potential for an online attack, system failure, data breach, or other event impacting an organization's information technology (IT) systems, and the potential consequences of that event, such as operational disruption, financial loss, or reputational damage (FSB 2018b)
data localization laws	Laws that restrict data flows across borders

decentralized finance (DeFi)	A set of alternative financial markets, products, and systems that operate using crypto-assets and "smart contracts" (software) built using distributed ledger or similar technology (FSB 2022)
deposit insurance	A system established to protect depositors against the loss of their insured deposits in the event that a bank cannot meet its obligations to the depositors ("Deposit Insurance," Glossary, International Association of Deposit Insurers website: https://www.iadi.org/en/core-principles-and -guidance/glossary/deposit-insurance/)
digital asset	A digital instrument that is issued or represented through the use of distributed ledger or similar technology, not including digital representations of fiat currencies (FSB 2022)
digital bank	Deposit-taking institutions that deliver banking services primarily through electronic channels instead of physical branches. They engage in risk transformation like traditional banks but have a technology-enabled business model and provide their services remotely with limited or no branch infrastructure (Ehrentraud, Ocampo, and Vega 2020). Digital banks are subject to all the typical prudential and regulatory frameworks applicable to traditional banks but might have some exemptions to account for their digital business model—for example, exemption from a required minimum number of physical bank branches or automated teller machines (ATMs).
digital financial services (DFS)	Financial products and services, including payments, transfers, savings, credit, insurance, securities, financial planning, and account statements that are delivered via digital or electronic technology such as e-money (initiated either online or on a mobile phone), payment cards, and a regular bank account
digital ID	A set of electronically captured and stored attributes and/ or credentials that uniquely identify a person. "Digital ID" also often refers to a digital identification (ID) system—an ID system that uses digital technology throughout the identity life cycle, including for data capture, validation, storage, and transfer; credential management; and identity verification and authentication.
digital literacy	The ability to define, access, manage, integrate, communicate, evaluate, and create information safely and appropriately through digital technologies and networked devices for participation in economic and social life (UIS and GAML 2018)

digital payments	Payment instructions that enter a payments system via the internet or other telecommunications network. The device used to initiate the payment could be a computer, mobile phone, point-of-service (POS) device, or any other device. The payment instrument used could be an e-money product, payment-card product, credit or debit transfer, or other innovative payment products.
distributed ledger technology (DLT)	A means of saving information through a distributed ledger—that is, a repeated digital copy of data available at multiple locations (FSB 2018a)
e-commerce	Buying and selling of goods or services using the internet
eKYC	Electronic Know Your Customer See also Know Your Customer (KYC).
electronic money institution	A legal person that has been granted authorization to issue electronic money
electronic signature or e-signature	An electronic sound, symbol, or process attached to or logically associated with a contract or other record and executed or adopted by a person with the intent to sign the record
embedded finance	The seamless incorporation of financial products or services into nonfinancial products or services See also contextualized finance.
emerging markets and developing economies (EMDEs)	Countries classified as "emerging markets and developing economies" by the IMF's *World Economic Outlook* (IMF 2020)
e-money or electronic money	Prepaid instrument that can be offered by banks and other authorized deposit-taking financial institutions, as well as by non-deposit-taking payment service providers such as mobile network operators. Depending on how these accounts are accessed, these could be further categorized as card-based e-money, mobile money, and online e-money (adapted from CPMI and World Bank Group 2016).
equity crowdfunding	Crowdfunding focused on equity instruments, without necessitating the traditional equity registration and listing process (adapted from Ehrentraud, Ocampo, and Vega 2020) See also crowdfunding.

factoring	A form of asset-based finance where the credit extended is based on the value of the borrower's accounts receivable—that is, the payments owed by the borrower's customers. In the small and medium enterprise (SME) context, factoring is a financing product that allows a financial institution to provide financing to an SME supplier through the purchase of its accounts receivable or invoices. See also reverse factoring.
fast payments	Payments in which the transmission of the payment message and the availability of final funds to the payee occur in real time or near-real time and on as near to a 24-hour and 7-day (24/7) basis as possible (CPMI 2016c)
Financial Action Task Force (FATF)	An intergovernmental body that sets international standards that aim to prevent and sanction money laundering, terrorism financing, and proliferation financing. As a policy-making body, the FATF works to generate the necessary political will to bring about national legislative and regulatory reforms in these areas ("Who We Are," FATF website: https://www.fatf-gafi .org/about/).
financial consumer protection (FCP)	The laws, regulations, and institutional arrangements that safeguard consumers in the financial marketplace of a given jurisdiction
financial inclusion	Individuals' and businesses' access to useful and affordable financial products and services that meet their needs—transactions, payments, savings, credit, and insurance—and are delivered in a responsible and sustainable way
financial intermediary	An entity that comes between two parties in a financial transaction, enabling transactions between parties without those parties having any direct relationship. Financial intermediaries channel funds between individuals or entities with surplus capital and those needing funds, and they may provide services such as maturity transformation, liquidity, risk diversification or redistribution, and monitoring. An example is a commercial bank that contracts separately with savers to obtain funds and with borrowers to lend those funds, often at a different maturity. Financial intermediaries include banks, investment banks, mutual and pension funds, broker-dealers, and insurance and leasing companies.

financial service provider (FSP)	Any entity or individual involved in providing financial services, including banks, nonbank financial institutions (NBFIs), insurance companies, e-money issuers, and payments providers
Financial Stability Board (FSB)	An international body that monitors and makes recommendations about the global financial system
fintech	Advances in technology that have the potential to transform the provision of financial services, spurring the development of new business models, applications, processes, and products (IMF and World Bank 2019). Examples include e-money, peer-to-peer lending, credit scoring and decisioning, robo-advisory services, and distributed ledger technology.
fintech firm (or a fintech)	A company that specializes in offering digital financial services. Fintech firms are also referred to as "fintechs" or "a fintech."
G-7 Fundamental Elements of Cybersecurity for the Financial Sector	A statement published in 2016 by the Group of Seven (G-7) that outlines fundamental principles for good cybersecurity in the financial services sector. The elements serve as the building blocks upon which an entity can design and implement its cybersecurity strategy and operating framework, informed by its approach to risk management and culture. The elements also provide steps in a dynamic process through which the entity can systematically reevaluate its cybersecurity strategy and framework as the operational and threat environment evolves. Public authorities within and across jurisdictions can use the elements as well to guide their public policy, regulatory, and supervisory efforts. Working together, informed by these elements, private and public entities and public authorities can help bolster the overall cybersecurity and resiliency of the international financial system.
global stablecoins	A stablecoin with a potential reach and adoption across multiple jurisdictions and the potential to achieve substantial volume See also stablecoin.
innovation facilitator	Public sector initiatives to engage with the fintech sector, such as regulatory sandboxes, innovation hubs, and innovation accelerators (FSB 2017b)

Internet of Things (IoT)	A system involving connected devices that gather data, connect with the internet or local networks, generate analytics, and (in some cases) adapt behavior or responses based on the data or analytics in the network. In the context of trade finance, for example, an IoT could track a shipment and automatically issue an invoice when the goods reach their destination. In the small and medium enterprise (SME) context, it can help monitor maintenance, sale, and restocking or replacement of collateral; automate settlement of agreements; and make asset-based financial products more affordable to both SMEs and financiers.
interoperability	Technical or legal compatibility that enables a system or mechanism to be used in conjunction with other systems or mechanisms. In the context of payments systems, interoperability allows customers of different payment service providers (PSPs) to be able to transact seamlessly as if they were customers of the same PSP (adapted from CPMI 2016b).
Know Your Customer (KYC)	Industry term for certain elements of the customer due diligence (CDD) requirements established by the Financial Action Task Force (FATF) and effectively implemented by countries' anti-money laundering and combating the financing of terrorism (AML/CFT) regimes. It commonly refers to a financial institution's process of identifying a customer and verifying the customer's identity at onboarding. More broadly, its uses may also include identifying the beneficial owners of customers that are "legal persons" (for example, corporations); understanding and obtaining information on the purpose and intended nature of the business relationship; conducting ongoing due diligence on that relationship; and monitoring the customer's transactions to ensure consistency with the financial institution's knowledge of the customer and risk profile.
machine learning (ML)	A subcategory of artificial intelligence, referring to a method of designing a sequence of actions to solve a problem, known as algorithms, that optimize automatically through experience and with limited or no human intervention (FSB 2017a) See also **artificial intelligence**.
mobile banking	Service provided by a bank or other financial service provider that allows customers to access a set of inquiry, transactional, and other services through their mobile devices. The range of services available could vary by jurisdiction and within a jurisdiction by provider.

mobile money	E-money product where the record of funds is stored on the mobile phone or a central computer system and that can be drawn down through specific payment instructions to be issued from the bearers' mobile phone
mobile payment	A type of e-payment, where the payment instrument used is a mobile money product See also mobile money.
mobile wallet	Service or product enabling a customer to access different bank and e-money accounts through a common interface on a mobile device. These services can be provided by a third party distinct from the institution holding the underlying accounts and may leverage different technologies—among others, application programming interfaces (APIs) and tokenization.
money transfer operator (MTO)	A non-deposit-taking payment service provider (PSP) where the service involves payment per transfer (or possibly payment for a set or series of transfers) by the sender *to* the PSP (for example, by cash or bank transfer)—that is, as opposed to a situation where the PSP debits an account held by the sender *at* the PSP
national payment system (NPS)	The configuration of diverse institutional arrangements and infrastructures that facilitate the transfer of monetary value between the parties in a transaction (CPMI 2006). An NPS can also be seen as the sum total of all the payment systems, payment instruments, and PSPs in a given jurisdiction.
neobank	A technology company offering banking or bank-like services. Use of "neo" denotes that these represent a new way to provide bank-like services without necessarily being licensed banks. In practice, some neobanks are licensed as PSPs, some as NBFIs, and others use a traditional bank or another PSP behind the scenes. Some notable fintech firms launched as neobanks and later obtained banking licenses, bringing them into the ranks of "challenger banks." See also digital bank.
nonbank financial institution (NBFI)	A financial institution that does not have a full banking license and cannot accept deposits from the public. NBFIs facilitate financial services such as investment (both collective and individual), leasing, consumer finance, risk pooling, financial consulting, brokering, money transmission, and check cashing.

open banking	Set of services that enables consumers and SMEs to share their bank and credit card transaction data securely with trusted third parties, who can then provide them with applications and financial services that save time and money (CMA 2021). It also enables consumers and SMEs to initiate payments directly from their payment accounts to the bank accounts of their payees, through interfaces and instruments provided by a third party and not the institution maintaining the account. Open banking uses application programming interfaces (APIs) extensively.
payment aggregator	A third-party institution that enables acquiring institutions (payment processing institutions) to reach smaller merchants. The third party maintains the direct relationship with the smaller merchants and handles much of the operations and servicing aspects (World Bank, forthcoming).
payment service provider (PSP)	An entity that provides payment services to end users: payers and payees. PSPs include banks and other deposit-taking institutions as well as specialized entities such as money transfer operators, e-money issuers, payment aggregators, and payment gateways.
peer-to-peer lending (P2PL)	A lending business model that uses online platforms to match potential lenders with borrowers See also crowdfunding.
Principles for Financial Market Infrastructures (PFMI)	International standards—issued by the Committee on Payments and Market Infrastructures (CPMI) and the International Organization of Securities Commissions (IOSCO)—for financial market infrastructures: payment systems that are systemically important, central securities depositories, securities settlement systems, central counterparties, and trade repositories (CPMI and IOSCO 2012)
real-time gross settlement (RTGS)	The real-time settlement of payments, transfer instructions, or other obligations individually on a transaction-by-transaction basis
regtech	Short form for "regulatory technology," which involves the use of new technologies to solve regulatory and compliance requirements more effectively and efficiently
regulatory arbitrage	A practice whereby firms capitalize on loopholes in regulatory systems to circumvent unfavorable regulations
remittances	Small-value, cross-border, person-to-person transfers

request to pay (RTP)	A payment instrument, represented by a set of instructions and rules, through which a merchant or other payee sends a payment request to the payer and the payer can authorize payment. Although the payee can initiate the request, the payer retains control over payment initiation and key aspects of transaction and account security. RTP is emerging in the context of open banking and faster payments systems as a way to provide the payer with the control required for security and finality in such systems, together with the convenience of merchant-initiated processing.
retail fast payment systems	Systems connecting PSPs that make funds available to the payee nearly instantaneously and can be used around-the-clock, seven days a week. Typically, such systems interconnect all the PSPs in a given jurisdiction and include various value-added services like alias-based payments, quick response (QR) codes, and application programming interface (API)-based payment services.
reverse factoring	A financing product by which a financial institution provides immediate liquidity to SMEs through the discounting of accounts payable of a large buyer, based on the buyer's credit risk
robo-advisory services	Automated, algorithm-driven financial planning services
sandbox or regulatory sandbox	In the regulatory context, a controlled, time-bound, live testing environment for a new technology or business model, which may feature regulatory waivers at regulators' discretion. The term originated in the information technology (IT) industry to refer to a segregated, isolated environment for testing products or software, thus mitigating risks before products were brought to market. Developers used IT sandboxes to execute suspicious code, launch stealth attacks, or check security software for vulnerabilities without risking harm to the host device or network.
software as a service (SaaS)	A method of software delivery and licensing in which software is accessed online via a subscription rather than bought and installed on individual computers (*Oxford English Dictionary*; Oxford Languages, https://languages.oup.com/). A range of services such as data processing, credit scoring, and electronic Know Your Customer (eKYC) may be provided to banks or other financial service providers (FSPs) via SaaS.
stablecoin	A crypto-asset that aims to maintain a stable value relative to a specified asset, or a pool or basket of assets (FSB 2022)

super-apps	Applications that encompass multiple different services and attempt to be a single point of entry and consolidation for a variety of user needs
suptech	Short for "supervisory technology," the use of technology-enabled solutions to increase the efficiency and effectiveness of supervisory activities
tokenization	This term is used in three different contexts:

tokenization (continued):

- Digital assets represented in a manner that enables peer-to-peer exchange without need for an intermediary institution maintaining record of ownership (see also digital assets).

- Digital representation of traditional assets—for example, financial instruments, a basket of collateral, or real assets—using technologies that can enable a peer-to-peer transfer (adapted from FSB 2019). The economic value and rights derived from these assets is embedded into the tokens.

- In the payment cards domain, to indicate provisioning of an alternate account identifier in a variety of devices that links back to the primary account identifier.

virtual asset	A digital representation of value that can be digitally traded, or transferred, and can be used for payment or investment purposes (FATF 2012–2022) See also crypto-assets, digital assets, and virtual-asset service provider (VASP).
virtual-asset service provider (VASP)	According to the Financial Action Task Force (FATF 2012–2022), a virtual-asset service provider (VASP) is any natural or legal person that, as a business, conducts one or more of the following activities or operations for or on behalf of another natural or legal person:

virtual-asset service provider (VASP) (continued):

- Exchange between virtual assets and fiat currencies

- Exchange between one or more forms of virtual assets

- Transfer of virtual assets

- Safekeeping and/or administration of virtual assets or instruments enabling control over virtual assets

- Participation in and provision of financial services related to an issuer's offer and/or sale of a virtual asset.

References

BCBS (Basel Committee on Banking Supervision). 2012. *Core Principles for Effective Banking Supervision.* Basel, Switzerland: Bank for International Settlements.

CMA (Competition and Markets Authority, United Kingdom). 2021. "Update on Open Banking." Corporate report, CMA, London.

CPMI (Committee on Payments and Market Infrastructures). 2006. *General Guidance for National Payment System Development.* Basel, Switzerland: Bank for International Settlements.

CPMI (Committee on Payments and Market Infrastructures). 2016a. *Correspondent Banking.* Basel, Switzerland: Bank for International Settlements.

CPMI (Committee on Payments and Market Infrastructures). 2016b. *A Glossary of Terms Used in Payments and Settlement Systems.* Rev. ed., updated 2016. Basel, Switzerland: Bank for International Settlements.

CPMI (Committee on Payments and Market Infrastructures). 2016c. *Fast Payments – Enhancing the Speed and Availability of Retail Payments.* Basel, Switzerland: Bank for International Settlements.

CPMI (Committee on Payments and Market Infrastructures). 2018. *Central Bank Digital Currencies.* Basel, Switzerland: Bank for International Settlements.

CPMI and IOSCO (Committee on Payments and Market Infrastructures and the International Organization of Securities Commissions). 2012. *Principles for Financial Market Infrastructures.* Basel, Switzerland: Bank for International Settlements; Madrid: IOSCO.

CPMI (Committee on Payments and Market Infrastructures) and World Bank Group. 2016. *Payment Aspects of Financial Inclusion.* Basel, Switzerland: Bank for International Settlements; Washington, DC: World Bank Group.

Didier, Tatiana, Erik Feyen, Ruth Llovet Montanes, and Oya Ardic. 2022. "Global Patterns of Fintech Activity and Enabling Factors." Fintech Activity Note for *Fintech and the Future of Finance*, World Bank, Washington, DC.

Ehrentraud, Johannes, Denise Garcia Ocampo, and Camila Quevedo Vega. 2020. *Regulating Fintech Financing: Digital Banks and Fintech Platforms.* Financial Stability Institute Insights on Policy Implementation No. 27. Basel, Switzerland: Bank for International Settlements.

FATF (Financial Action Task Force). 2012–2022. "International Standards on Combating Money Laundering and the Financing of Terrorism & Proliferation: The FATF Recommendations." FATF, Paris.

FSB (Financial Stability Board). 2017a. "Artificial Intelligence and Machine Learning in Financial Services: Market Developments and Financial Stability Implications." Report, FSB, Basel, Switzerland.

FSB (Financial Stability Board). 2017b. "Financial Stability Implications from FinTech: Supervisory and Regulatory Issues that Merit Authorities' Attention." Report, FSB, Basel, Switzerland.

FSB (Financial Stability Board). 2018a. "Crypto-Asset Markets: Potential Channels for Future Financial Stability Implications." Report, FSB, Basel, Switzerland.

FSB (Financial Stability Board). 2018b. "Cyber Lexicon." FSB, Basel, Switzerland.

FSB (Financial Stability Board). 2019. "Decentralised Financial Technologies: Report on Financial Stability, Regulatory and Governance Implications." Report, FSB, Basel, Switzerland.

FSB (Financial Stability Board). 2020a. "Addressing the Regulatory, Supervisory, and Oversight Challenges Raised by the 'Global Stablecoin' Arrangements." Consultative document, FSB, Basel, Switzerland.

FSB (Financial Stability Board). 2020b. "Enhancing Cross-Border Payments: Stage 1 Report to the G20." Technical background report, FSB, Basel, Switzerland.

FSB (Financial Stability Board). 2021. "Targets for Addressing the Four Challenges of Cross-Border Payments: Final Report." FSB, Basel, Switzerland.

FSB (Financial Stability Board). 2022. "Assessment of Risks to Financial Stability from Crypto-Assets." Report, FSB, Basel, Switzerland.

IMF (International Monetary Fund). 2018. "The Bali Fintech Agenda." Policy paper, October 11, IMF, Washington, DC.

IMF (International Monetary Fund). 2020. "Country Composition of WEO Groups," Database of WEO Groups and Aggregates Information, *World Economic Outlook, April 2020: The Great Lockdown.* Washington, DC: IMF.

IMF (International Monetary Fund) and World Bank. 2019. "Fintech: The Experience So Far." Policy Paper No. 2019/024, IMF and World Bank, Washington, DC.

UIS and GAML (UNESCO Institute for Statistics and Global Alliance to Monitor Learning). 2018. "A Global Framework of Reference on Digital Literacy Skills for Indicator 4.4.2." Draft report for the Digital Literacy Global Framework, UIS, Montreal.

World Bank. 2011. "General Principles for Credit Reporting." Report No. 70193, World Bank, Washington, DC.

World Bank. Forthcoming. "Electronic Payments Acceptance Toolkit." Toolkit, World Bank, Washington, DC.